Natural Pregnancy and Birth

The chapter on Healthy Living contains practical, common-sense advice on how to protect yourself and baby from unnecessary exposure to harmful chemicals and pollutants in the home environment as well as the workplace. In addition, there's general advice, such as how to eat healthily and how to ensure your physical and emotional well-being, so you can enjoy your pregnancy to the full.

This book aims to give you useful information about your pre-conceptual and antenatal care, and preparation for labour, birth and the early post-natal period. It is wonderful that you are informing yourself on these issues so you can make confident decisions. However, I also believe that mums-to-be instinctively know what is right for them and their unborn child and, as a starting point in all pregnancy matters, you should trust your intuition.

The contents of this book are by no means exhaustive, but there should be more than enough practical suggestions here to guide you through a natural, comfortable and rewarding pregnancy that leads to a happy and healthy baby and lays the foundation for a green and healthy future for your new family.

Contents

Foreword

by Annie Francis, Board Member of Independent Midwives UK

Independent Midwives UK is a national organization whose mission is to support its members in providing culturally safe, empowering and supportive midwifery care. Each independent midwife aims to work in partnership with women and their families, giving individualized care based on continuity and trust. This book reflects their ethos and values in its focus on a natural, healthy approach to the unique and life-changing event of childbirth.

Pregnancy is a very special time. It offers women the opportunity to rethink their priorities and to make changes to their lifestyle in preparation for the challenges and joys of parenthood. The potential for shifts in thinking is explored in the early chapters: Claire highlights the importance of intuition, relaxation and emotional well-being. She discusses how to ensure a healthy lifestyle through diet – the section on superfoods is inspiring. Managing the work environment and creating a green home are all topics which Claire addresses from a balanced and sensible viewpoint.

The need for every woman to gather information to help make the right choice for her is a constant refrain throughout this book. However, it is the emphasis on the importance of her taking responsibility for those decisions and growing in confidence as she does so which is so refreshing. There can sometimes be a tendency for maternity care to be paternalistic in its approach, for the system to take over and, on occasion, railroad women into making inappropriate decisions they feel uncomfortable with. Claire helps to counteract this trend using a friendly, non-judgemental style.

Independent midwives relish the freedom they have to truly work with women, supporting them through the often complex and bewildering array of options on offer, to arrive at a conclusion which feels comfortable and 'right'. This book complements that process perfectly and, when continuity is not always available, can work well on its own, prompting areas for discussion with her caregiver which enable a woman to tease out the important issues for her.

The chapter on birth options is particularly valuable for those women seeking a more natural approach to birth. Independent midwives understand the crucial importance of good support through the challenges of labour – evidence shows that when it comes from a known caregiver, it will greatly increase the chances of a straightforward, empowering birth experience, reducing the need for medical pain relief and other interventions. Claire presents a balanced view on the benefits of home birth and what forms of natural pain relief are available. All these factors can help ensure the woman feels comfortable and relaxed, which, in turn, reduces the hormones which interfere with labour and maximizes those which help it progress.

These same hormones, especially oxytocin, are in plentiful supply immediately after the baby is born following a natural, drug-free labour. Although bonding is a very personal and individual process, there is no doubt that this magical hormone can aid the process beautifully, both around the time of birth and during every breast feed – as good a reason as any to aim for as green and natural a birth as possible.

Annie Francis
www.independentmidwives.org.uk

Introduction

Finding out that you are expecting a baby is such monumental news. It can be joyous, shocking, overwhelming, but always of huge significance, and probably the biggest life-changing event you will ever experience. It seems to me that there is never a better time than when you are pregnant to embrace a greener approach to life, your body and our planet.

By investigating and seeking natural products, non-invasive treatments and drug-free approaches to pregnancy and birth, you are actively taking steps to ensure a happy and healthy conclusion to your pregnancy, namely a hale and hearty baby.

The aim of this book is to help you to enjoy your pregnancy in the most natural way possible and in a manner that fits in with your particular beliefs and lifestyle. It is written with all women in mind, regardless of how much or little you want to adopt a natural approach. Some of you will be keen to espouse the vast majority of the advice contained in these pages; others will be happy to cherry-pick the suggestions that best resonate with you. Either way is fine.

Of course, what we now call a natural pregnancy and active birth used to be the norm. It was only during the twentieth century, with the ascendance of medical doctors and obstetricians, that it was decided that pregnancy and childbirth needed greater monitoring and more medical intervention. Although still less than 1 per cent of American babies and only 2.7 per cent of British babies are born at home, these figures are on the increase, and there appears to be a sea-change in women's attitudes to how their pregnancy and birth are handled. More and more women are keen to take back ownership and responsibility for their antenatal health and to be less passive in giving birth to their babies.

That is not to say that modern medicine does not have its place and this book is certainly not anti-medical. Indeed, thanks to advances in allopathic medicines and obstetric care, premature babies born as young as 24 weeks now stand a very good chance of survival. And in an emergency or an out-of-the-ordinary pregnancy, the medical treatment you will receive is often essential and potentially life-saving.

My point is that the vast majority of pregnancies and births are not emergencies. They are low-risk and, as such, both mother and baby can benefit from a more natural approach. Your body is perfectly capable of sustaining a blooming and joyful pregnancy and supporting the healthy growth and development of your unborn child. By being prepared and informed about your birth options, you can approach labour with a sense of control and confidence, too.

The information in this book aims to give you choice and the confidence to take control over your body. Most pregnant women are reluctant to pop a pill that might have unexpected side effects, but there is no need to suffer during pregnancy. The chapter on Remedies and Therapies guides you through a host of natural therapies that are suitable and safe during pregnancy, and complementary therapies and natural self-help remedies are suggested in chapter 7 that can see you comfortably through many of the common pregnancy ailments.

You can prepare yourself emotionally for the life-changing events of pregnancy, birth and looking after your newborn baby, too. Your pregnancy is a perfect time during which you can build a relationship between yourself and the baby in your womb, who is aware and sensitive to your moods and feelings. This forms a loving platform on which you can build your future relationship with your son or daughter.

A GREEN GUIDE TO YOUR

Natural Pregnancy and Birth

the kind way for you, your baby and the environment

claire gillman

Foreword by Annie Francis, Independent Midwives UK

CICO BOOKS

LONDON NEW YORK

This book is dedicated to the woman who carried me so well for nine months – my lovely mum, Eileen May Gillman.

Published in 2010 by CICO Books
an imprint of Ryland Peters & Small
20–21 Jockey's Fields, London WC1R 4BW

www.cicobooks.com

10 9 8 7 6 5 4 3 2 1

A CIP catalogue record for this book is available from the British Library.

ISBN-13: 978-1-907030-56-7

Printed in China

Copy editor: Katie Hardwicke
Designer: Barbara Zuñiga

Please note that the advice in this book is not to be considered as a substitute for medical advice from your family doctor or any other qualified medical practitioner. If you treat yourself with natural medicines, such as herbs, you should always inform your doctor, because these can be very powerful and can interact with prescribed and over-the-counter medications.

Your Pregnancy Milestones

The week-by-week calendar in this chapter (see pages 14–19) charts the many changes that you can expect in your body and emotions as you progress through each trimester of your pregnancy. Alongside, you will find a guide to how your baby begins to develop and grow inside. Some of the changes to you, especially the physical ones, are very obvious but you may be less sensible to other, more subtle alterations. Meanwhile, your baby's milestones are reached on an almost weekly basis and are quite astonishingly remarkable.

The illustrated monthly timeline (see pages 12–13) takes you step-by-step from the moment of conception to the birth of your new baby so that you can see at a glance how you might look plus what might be happening in your life at that particular stage of your pregnancy. It's both reassuring, comforting and yet strangely exciting to be able to see what comes next – so enjoy!

Pregnancy Week-by-week

This month-by-month calendar pictorially charts the progress in one woman's pregnancy. You may notice many of the same changes in your body and emotions as you move towards your due date.

The 40 weeks of pregnancy are calculated from the first day of your last menstrual period. After conception, your baby actually only takes 38 weeks to develop. So, when using these milestones (and the ones on the following pages), do bear in mind that there is some leeway in how far along you are in your pregnancy, depending on whether or not your menstrual cycle is an exact 28 days. However, this chart will give you a general idea of the stage of growth that your baby is at.

Pregnancy Timeline

Month 1
Whether you've taken a home pregnancy test or been to your doctor to confirm the news, it will take a little while for it to sink in. However, it's surprising how many women know or suspect they've conceived before a urine test confirms the news.

Month 2
Although you look the same, you may be feeling very different. It's entirely up to you when you decide to share your news with friends and loved ones, but this stage when it's just a secret between you and your partner can feel very special and intimate.

Month 3
The physical discomforts of early pregnancy should be wearing off but you'll need a proper maternity bra about now. You might want to start thinking about telling your employer and enrolling for antenatal exercise classes.

Month 4
As you start to feel much better, now's the time to get excited. You may need to get some natural-fibre maternity clothes too as your ordinary clothes will probably become too tight at this stage.

Month 5
Many women report a sense of well-being at this stage and are often described as 'radiant,' due to improvements in skin and hair. You should be enjoying the thrill of feeling your baby move around now.

Conception

You are most fertile about 14 days before your period is due. At this time, a ripe egg is released from one of your ovaries. It travels down the Fallopian tube and, if not fertilized, it passes out of the vagina along with the womb lining, as your next period.

However, if a sperm successfully enters the egg during its journey down the tube, fertilization takes place and the egg and sperm fuse together to form a single cell. It continues to divide as it travels down the Fallopian tube. On about the fourth day after fertilization, the egg reaches the womb. By now, it is a ball of about 100 cells and for the next few days, it floats freely in the womb. After about three weeks, the fertilized egg attaches itself to the soft lining of the womb. The egg sends projections into the lining of the womb that eventually join up with the mother's blood vessels and form the elementary beginnings of the placenta.

greenfile

Remember, every pregnancy is unique and your experiences may differ greatly from those of your friends or text books.

Month 6
This is the month where you start to pile on the pounds and most women appear visibly pregnant by now. Pay attention to your posture and practise gentle exercise together with relaxation and breathing techniques.

Month 7
You're probably starting to feel large and clumsy, and are possibly growing more forgetful. Don't forget to let your employer know in writing when you intend to stop work. You're entering the home straight now.

Month 8
As your body prepares for the birth, you will need as much rest as possible so take naps if you are not sleeping as well as usual. Now is the time to start attending antenatal classes if you haven't already done so and buying baby essentials – what fun!

Month 9
The 'nesting instinct' is often strong, so don't be surprised if you find yourself cleaning out cupboards and tidying the house. Buy your nursing bras and check everything is ready for the baby. By now, you are probably impatient to give birth and the wait is almost over.

First Trimester

**Your Baby's
Milestones**

Weeks 1–3
Six or seven days after fertilization, the developing cell mass, known as a blastocyst, becomes embedded in the uterus where it multiplies fast.

Weeks 4–6
By week 4, your baby is about 2 mm ($\frac{1}{16}$ in) long and weighs less than 1 g ($\frac{1}{4}$ oz). Body tissues are starting to form and at week 5, the heart has started to develop.

Week 6
Now an embryo, your baby's heart is beating at about 180 beats per minute. It has eyelids, ears and the beginnings of hands and feet. The head and the curve of the spine can be distinguished.

Week 7
It is starting to move its body, arms and legs, although you cannot feel the movements yet. The nervous system, lungs, kidney and liver are starting to develop.

**Your Pregnancy
Timeline**

First Trimester
Up to Week 12
In the early weeks of pregnancy you may experience:
• Enlarged, tender breasts that may tingle slightly
• A strange metallic taste in your mouth
• Feeling rather emotional and easily upset because of hormonal changes
• A frequent need to pass water
• Nausea and perhaps vomiting at any time of the day, even though it's called 'morning sickness'
• Tiredness
• Feeling faint and dizzy
• A strong dislike of certain tastes, especially tea, coffee, alcohol, toothpaste and cigarettes, but a craving for others
• An increase in normal vaginal discharge

Week 8

At this stage, your baby has evolved into a foetus that is about 2.5 cm (1 in) in length. It can open and close its mouth, and ears are beginning to form. Its brain is developing rapidly.

Week 9

Your baby is now 4 cm (1½ in) long and its brain has quadrupled in size in the past four weeks.

Week 10

Your baby now looks like a miniature human being and all its organs are fully formed. The amniotic sac has formed and your baby is moving around more because its nervous system is more mature (but you won't feel it yet).

Week 11

Now about 5 cm (2 in) long, your baby has a fully formed face and its liver and kidneys are beginning to function.

Week 12

Remarkably, your baby is now fully formed, although it's only 6 cm (2½ in) long. Its nails and hair are starting to grow, it has all 32 teeth buds and it is starting to suck. His or her sex organs have now formed.

Week 12

You may find that:
• You feel less nauseous
• You don't need to pass water quite so often
• You get constipated as bowel movements tend to become sluggish during pregnancy
• You cease to feel the cold because the volume of blood circulating in your body increases

Second Trimester

Your Baby's Timeline

Week 13
Your baby's body is growing rapidly and s/he is supported by the placenta.

Week 14
Your baby can discern sound and light and responds to touch. S/he will swallow amniotic fluid and excrete it. The limbs are fully formed.

Week 15
Your baby is moving more vigorously now and the bones are hardening. As s/he becomes more active, you may start to notice movement – often a light, fluttering sensation – particularly when you're resting.

Week 16
Your baby now has fingerprints and is covered in a downy hair all over the body, known as lanugo. Nipples appear and the back, which has been curved, straightens.

Week 17
Your baby is about 18 cm (7 in) long and weighs about 170 g (6 oz). S/he has facial expressions and eyelashes, and eyebrows are developing.

Your Pregnancy Timeline

Week 16
You may find that:
• You're feeling much better
• Your nipples and the areola may darken and a faint line, called the linea nigra, may appear down the centre of your stomach – this fades after the birth
• You may no longer be able to fit into your ordinary clothes

Weeks 18–20

Your baby may start to suck its thumb. The spinal cord is thickening and by the end of this period, s/he will have reached roughly half its length at birth. Hair is growing on the head and the rate of growth starts to slow.

Weeks 21–23

Your baby has taste buds and the ears are fully formed so s/he can hear and respond to music, sounds and your speaking/singing /crying etc. Your baby can also grip with the hands and may occasionally grasp the umbilical cord.

Week 24

S/he can open the eyes and identify voices. The heartbeat may now be discernible by fetoscope and will usually range between 120 and 160 beats per minute. The skin is translucent and blood vessels can be clearly seen through it.

Weeks 25–26

The baby has wakeful and sleeping periods. S/he is covered in vernix – a white, waxy substance that nourishes and waterproofs the skin.

Week 27

This sees the start of another growth spurt and your baby will start to put on weight.

Week 20

You may find that:
- You feel great, even radiant, as you pass into the middle months of the pregnancy
- Your breasts may produce small amounts of colostrum, which is a clear, thin liquid
- Physical reactions may include bleeding gums and vaginal discharge
- Your joints and ligaments have relaxed so you are more prone to back trouble and aches and pains
- You may get patches of pigmentation on your face and body – these will fade after the birth
- Your nails split and break more easily

Week 24

You may find that:
- Your bump is growing rapidly
- You look a little puffy as your body retains more water
- You sweat more as you feel the heat
- You have a sudden weight gain

Third Trimester

Your Baby's Timeline

Week 28
If born now, although not fully matured, your baby would have a good chance of survival. Your baby's eyes are beginning to be able to focus and, if it's a boy, his testes have now descended into the groin.

Week 29
Your baby is now around 34 cm (13½ in) long. The lungs have developed alveoli and are also producing a wetting agent, known as surfactant, to assist breathing at birth.

Week 30
Expect lots of movement now because your baby has increased muscle tone.

Week 31
Your baby has been gaining weight at a rate of about 250 g (8 oz) a week. As fat deposits are laid down, so its skin begins to smooth out and become pink rather than red.

Weeks 32–33
Fingernails are fully grown (but not toenails) and the face has plumped out. Although your baby appears as you would expect to see at birth, its body systems are still maturing.

Your Pregnancy Timeline

Week 28
You may find that:
• You get short of breath, heartburn, indigestion and cramps
• Stretch marks may appear on your stomach
• The veins on your breasts may become more pronounced
• You may put weight on your buttocks and thighs as well as your stomach
• You are having vivid and possibly frightening dreams. This is quite common and nothing to worry about. The dreams are not portentous but a product of your disturbed sleep

Week 32
You may find that:
• The pressure on your internal organs makes you breathless and need to pass urine frequently. You may find you leak a little urine when you cough, sneeze, laugh or run
• Your navel may have flattened or popped out
• You may be experiencing sleeping problems
• The base of your ribcage may be sore as the womb presses up under it
• You may experience discomfort in the pelvic region as the joints expand ready for the birth

Weeks 34–35

The immune system is still developing and your baby continues to receive your antibodies. However, the brain and nervous system are now fully developed. Your baby is about 37 cm (14½ in) in length and weighs about 2 kg (4 lb). As your baby becomes more cramped in its space, s/he may start to move less.

Week 36

Meconium, a thick, green liquid consisting of dead cells and secretions from the liver and bowel, is beginning to form in the intestines (this will be your baby's first motion). If your baby was born now, s/he should be mature enough to survive without too much difficulty.

Week 37

Your baby is rehearsing how to breathe, suck and swallow. All of the sense organs are formed and s/he is ready for life outside of your womb. The baby has lost most of the lanugo and vernix that covered its body.

Week 38

Your baby is ready to be born. S/he is about 46–50 cm (18–21 in) long and weighs on average between 2.7–4 kg (6–9 lb). There is very little room inside the uterus and s/he has to curl up tightly. The head has now descended into the lower part of your pelvis, ready for birth.

Week 36

You may find that:
• Some of the more unpleasant symptoms, such as breathlessness, heartburn and indigestion, lessen as the baby's head drops into the pelvis
• You pass water a great deal
• You're tired and irritable
• You're apprehensive about the birth but want the pregnancy to be over
• The 'nesting instinct' is strong. You have bursts of energy during which you clear out cupboards and prepare the home

Week 40

You may find that:
• You have pins and needles in your legs
• You can't move around very easily
• Your lower abdomen feels drawn and heavy
• You experience Braxton Hicks contractions (also known as false labour)
• You lose a little weight or your weight gain tails off. This is a sign that the baby is full term

A Healthy Start

Discovering that you are pregnant is such a momentous and exciting moment. However, like any major life event, once the news has settled in, you can sometimes experience a mixture of emotions. This is perfectly natural. While in western society, we place a great deal of emphasis on the obvious physical changes of pregnancy (see the illustrated monthly timeline on pages 12–13), in eastern philosophy, it is equally important that you pay attention to your emotional and spiritual well-being (see page 32) and that you learn to listen intuitively to your body and its changes (see page 31).

In holistic circles, you hear people speak of the twelve months of pregnancy. Although it is commonly accepted that the physical growth of the baby takes only nine months, many consider the few months before conception to be as important as the nine months term during which the foetus grows inside the womb. This is because, with good pre-conceptual preparation, your baby will get the best start it can towards a healthy life (see page 22).

So, this chapter is devoted to making sure that you nurture yourself throughout the 'twelve months' of pregnancy, keeping yourself healthy and well (see page 26), keeping your relationship strong (see page 34) and keeping yourself relaxed and stress-free (see page 36).

Pregnancy is a wonderful time despite the discomforts that are sometimes associated with it, and it offers a glorious opportunity for you to plan and think about the sort of parent(s) you might like to be.

Pre-conceptual Health

After spending years worrying about contraception, it is one of life's bitter ironies that some couples then find it difficult to conceive when they eventually decide to have a baby.

In fact, for conception to take place successfully, you need a good foundation. You both need to be as fit and healthy as possible before trying to conceive if you are to:
- optimize the chances of conceiving
- reduce the risk of miscarriage
- improve the probability of carrying a pregnancy to full-term
- increase the likelihood of delivering a healthy baby

In particular, the three-to-six-month period prior to conception plays a vital role in your baby's future, both physically and intellectually, and so it is important that both partners start preparing for a pregnancy at least three months before you want to conceive.

Lifestyle Changes
It is now known that health and lifestyle affect the fertility of both parents. If you have a pressurized job and lead a hectic social life, you may need to make a few adjustments.

It is recommended that both partners give up alcohol, smoking and recreational drugs some months before trying to conceive. Street drugs, in particular cannabis, are known to reduce sperm production significantly, and the effects can take a considerable time to wear off. Tobacco affects the motility of the sperm (active movement), while alcohol increases the number of dead and deformed sperm. Not only does this reduce your chances of conception but it also increases the risks of miscarriage, should you be lucky enough to conceive, because an egg fertilized by a damaged sperm is more likely to be rejected by your body.

Obviously, the effects on the foetus from alcohol and tobacco consumption are well documented but it is less well known that smoking reduces female fertility – an American study by the National Institute of Environmental Health showed that female non-smokers were more than three times more likely to conceive than smokers. Moreover, it is believed that alcohol inhibits the passage of the egg from the ovary to the womb, again adversely affecting female fertility.

The best advice is to give up drinking and smoking completely but, if this is too much of a tall order for you, at least cut down on your consumption, with a view to eventually giving up if possible (see pages 52 and 72).

Reducing Stress Levels
If you are stressed in your work or simply a naturally tense person, you may experience difficulty in getting pregnant. In women, stress is thought to interfere with ovulation, while in men, stress hormones inhibit sperm production.

In extreme cases, you may decide that it's worth changing your job, depending on how much your work is affecting your health. Usually, it is enough to invest time in learning techniques for stress management, in slowing down the pace of your lifestyle, and/or in using complementary therapies, such as aromatherapy massage or herbal remedies, to relax (see pages 106 and 112).

greenfile
Neroli, rose or sandalwood essential oils can help to calm and relax. Essential oils, such as chamomile, lavender and geranium, are good if you're feeling irritable and tense.

Good Nutrition

Both prospective parents need a nutritious diet to produce healthy sperm and eggs, which in turn will produce a healthy foetus. Make an effort to include as much fresh fruit and vegetables, and meat and fish, in your diet as possible, plus plenty of wholegrain breads and cereals.

Vitamins and minerals are particularly important at this time, so if you find it difficult to eat a nutrient-rich diet, you should consider taking a multi-vitamin and mineral supplement (see page 58).

One of the key nutrients of paramount importance to women hoping to get pregnant is folic acid. A lack of folic acid in the diet can increase the risk of having a baby with spina bifida or other neural tube defects. So you should increase your intake of this important nutrient at least three months before you try to conceive and continue well into the pregnancy (for the first trimester at least). For natural sources of folic acid see page 44, and for supplements, see page 58.

Contraception

If you use hormone-based contraception, such as the Pill, most doctors recommend that you switch to a barrier method for about three months before trying to conceive. This allows your natural fertility cycle to re-establish itself – although it can take up to a year – and vitamin and mineral levels to return to normal. While on the Pill, the amount of folic acid, vitamin C, vitamin E and zinc in your blood are reduced, while iron and copper levels are raised. There's no direct evidence that this harms a developing foetus but it may affect fertility. If you are fitted with an intra-uterine contraceptive device (IUCD or coil), have this removed at least a month before you plan to conceive.

Indeed, if it is taking you longer than you had hoped or expected to conceive, the pressure of trying to get pregnant can, in itself, be stressful. Try not to be disappointed if you don't see immediate results. As a generalization, nearly half of all couples trying to conceive are successful within six months, a further 35 per cent take up to a year and the remaining 15 per cent take longer and may need medical intervention. However, your doctor is unlikely to take any action with regard to infertility investigations unless you have been trying to conceive for at least a year and, in some cases, eighteen months.

So, although it may sound trite to say so, try not to be tense about getting pregnant. The more uptight you get each month that goes by, the harder it will be for you to conceive.

Medical Conditions

Symptomless genito-urinary infections can impede conception and increase the risk of miscarriage and premature labour. Chlamydia is a common infection that often goes undetected, yet it can adversely affect your newborn baby, so it's worth getting yourself tested.

You should also let your doctor know that you are planning to conceive so that he can monitor any prescription drugs s/he might normally prescribe. For example, antibiotics and certain asthma treatments can affect both male and female fertility, and you should always speak to the pharmacist before buying over-the-counter drugs during the three months prior to trying to conceive.

Finally, for women who have never had German measles (rubella) and who are uncertain about their vaccinations, it is important to ask your doctor for a blood test to check your immunity. If you contract rubella during pregnancy, it can damage your unborn child and cause serious birth defects. If you have no immunity, it is well worth getting the vaccination, but make sure you do so at least three months before trying to conceive.

greenfile

False unicorn root (*Chamaelirium luteum*) is recommended for both men and women planning to conceive as it strengthens and tones the reproductive system. It is available in capsule or tincture form, and the root or liquid extract can also be taken in a tea.

Age

A woman is at the peak of her fertility in her mid-twenties. Thereafter, her fertility starts to decrease and the decline is particularly acute after the age of 35. A man's fertility levels, on the other hand, stay pretty constant until he reaches his early fifties and, biologically speaking, men are perfectly capable of fathering a child well into their eighties.

Timing

Make love as often as you like without getting too hung up on whether or not it's the right stage of your

---

BEFORE YOU CONCEIVE

Both you and your partner should:
- Give up smoking and recreational drugs
- Give up alcohol
- Eat a healthy, nutritious diet
- Reduce stress
- Check for genito-urinary infections
- Monitor prescription drug use
- Take regular exercise, but not at excessive levels

You should:
- Stop using contraceptives
- Take extra folic acid (see page 23)
- Check immunity to rubella
- Avoid X-rays

YOUR PARTNER:
The testes need to be several degrees cooler than body temperature because sperm production takes place at 32ºC (89ºF) – normal body temperature is 37ºC (98.4ºF).

He should:
- Wear loose fitting underwear and trousers
- Avoid sitting for long periods and avoid crossing legs
- Avoid hot baths and electric blankets
- Turn the central heating down
- Seek advice if you are in a hazardous occupation, such as working with radiation, for example dentists and X-ray technicians, or using chemicals at work, for example farmers or dry cleaners

cycle. There is actually a three- or four-day period in the middle of your cycle (an egg is released from the ovary about 12–16 days before the next expected period and this is your most fertile time) during which time you could conceive, so you don't have to leap on each other at the exact moment of ovulation.

Making love according to temperatures and calendars can, in itself, be stressful and is certainly a turn off. If you make love regularly three or so times a week, you will be doing enough to make conception likely to happen.

A Pre-conception Visit

A check-up is not necessary for everyone but you should see your GP if there is anything you want to discuss or if you have a chronic health problem that needs treatment. A visit can be useful in recognizing factors that might affect the timing or your decision to become pregnant, particularly in the case of women with significant health problems, such as diabetes, epilepsy and congenital heart disease, and for couples with genetic risk factors.

A pre-conception appointment will provide:

- Risk assessment based on your medical histories, nutritional state and personal/social issues
- Assessment of genetic concerns, with possible referral for genetic testing or counselling before pregnancy
- Immunization checks and updates
- Risk of Hepatitis B assessment
- Laboratory testing, if you have concerns about HIV, for example
- Contraception advice

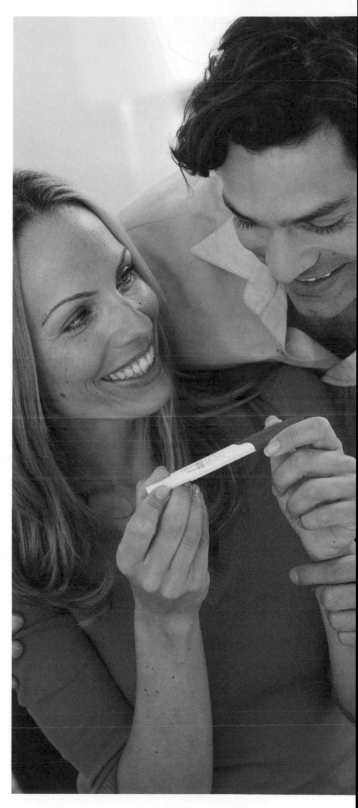

greenfile

Although you can buy over-the-counter ovulation test kits, if you know your body well, you can detect your time of ovulation naturally: fluid from the vagina becomes thinner and wetter at this time, which is a good indication of ovulation.

Taking Care of Yourself

Whatever stage of life, your health should always be an important consideration but it is likely that you will be more conscious about keeping healthy during your pregnancy than at any other time.

In part, that's because you know that if you fall ill, you may not be able to take the medications that you would normally resort to. However, it is also because you want to give your baby the very best start in life – and staying healthy is integral to that goal.

From a more selfish perspective, research shows that healthier mothers have shorter labours and recover faster after the birth. So, not only is staying healthy during pregnancy important for your unborn child's development, it's also in your best interests too!

Moreover, a healthy pregnancy lays the foundation of health to support you through your baby's early years. Remember, a well-nourished, healthy mother is better able to cope with the stresses of early parenthood than one who is unhealthy.

So, how do you maintain good health throughout your pregnancy? The answer is not as complex as you might think. With a combination of nutritious eating and smart lifestyle choices, you are giving yourself the very best chance to stay healthy throughout your nine-month term.

Nutritious Eating

The following chapter (see page 42) is devoted to giving you the necessary nutritional information to make sure that your baby gets everything that it needs to grow and develop healthily and to keep you in optimum health.

However, it's worth pointing out here that, even when you are eating the right foods, there are still further ways that you can help yourself to stay healthy. For example, it's better for your digestive system to eat four to six smaller meals per day rather than three big ones. This is due to the fact that your stomach is being compressed by your growing baby and cannot hold as much food as it might normally.

So, even if you're eating nutritiously, by eating little and often, you are helping your digestive system to remain healthy. This simple solution can help you to avoid one of pregnancy's most common ailments – heartburn (see page 122).

By the same token, you can reduce the likelihood of heartburn if you stay away from foods that you find hard to digest. These foods are, of course, peculiar to the individual and you will know what yours are, but heartburn is more of a problem in pregnancy because your small and large intestines wrap around the uterus, so digestion takes longer than usual.

> *greenfile*
>
> **To aid good digestion and to keep your body hydrated, you should drink at least eight glasses of liquid each day, preferably in the form of water, milk, unsweetened fruit juices, and fruit, herbal or green tea.**

Pregnancy Exercise

A great way to stay healthy during your pregnancy is to maintain your fitness levels with safe, gentle exercise.

According to the American Congress of Obstetricians and Gynecologists (ACOG), regular exercise can:

- Ease backaches, constipation, bloating and swelling
- Help to prevent or treat gestational diabetes
- Increase your energy
- Improve your mood
- Improve your posture
- Promote muscle tone, strength and endurance
- Help you to sleep better
- Improve your ability to cope with the pain of labour
- Make it easier for your to get back in shape after the birth

Boosting Your Immunity

During pregnancy, your natural immunity is slightly lowered (in order to prevent your body rejecting the developing baby), which means that you will find you are more susceptible to illnesses, such as recurrent coughs and colds, fatigue and bacterial, viral or fungal infections.

There are a number of factors that can cause you to have a weakened immune system. For example, stress and anxiety depress the immune system, as does inadequate rest. A poor diet also deprives the body of the necessary nutrients to maintain a healthy immune system. Less well known is the fact that long-term use of antibiotics can cause impairment of the immune system.

You can help to boost your immune system by avoiding the above triggers and by eating foods rich in vitamins A, C and E, zinc and selenium (see pages 44–47 for natural food sources). These nutrients enhance your immune system and help the production of specialized white blood cells, which are mobilized to attack when a pathogen invades the body.

Complementary therapies, such as acupuncture, aromatherapy and herbal remedies, can also be beneficial in supporting your body's immunity (see pages 101–117).

However, you must be fairly sensible about exercising during pregnancy. Most forms of exercise are safe but, if you're new to exercise, choose a gentle, low-impact sport, such as swimming, walking, antenatal aerobics, aqua aerobics, yoga or pilates.

If you are already a regular sportswoman, then it should be safe to continue with your chosen activity, although it is worth discussing this with your health practitioner first. Naturally, contact or extreme sports should be avoided. If your sport involves a risk of falling, for example horse riding or water-skiing, you might be best advised to wait until after the birth to resume your activities.

Remember your new shape and body mass coupled with the fact that the ligaments throughout your body are relaxed and joints are less stable, means that you should take care not to push yourself excessively or beyond what feels comfortable when exercising during pregnancy.

Beating Stress

In our modern age, it is almost impossible to avoid stress altogether. However, when you are pregnant, it is important to minimize your exposure to stressful factors as much as possible if you and your growing baby are to remain healthy. Stress not only adversely affects your body and health, but it affects the baby by flooding his body with the stress hormone cortisol, which can increase the rate of his heartbeat and raise his blood pressure. At the same time, stress can cause your body to suffer muscle cramps and increased heart rate, among other problems.

So, make a concerted effort to slow your life down, to focus your attention on you and your baby, and to relax. You will find a number of recommended relaxation techniques later in this chapter (see page 36), but it is also useful to make a special space for yourself at this time where you can feel safe and secure and in which you can take refuge from life's daily stresses.

Why not set aside a room or an area of your bedroom where you can seek sanctuary. Light the special space with your favourite candles. Surround yourself with the scents that relax you – fragrant potpourri, incense, aromatherapy oils, scented candles or fragrant bubble baths.

And finally, music is a subtle yet powerful way to affect your mood. You can use music to release mental energy and to relax tension in your body. Whatever your particular favourite, whether it's uplifting rock or atmospheric spiritual chants, find something that helps you to unwind and beat the stress of everyday life.

If you don't have family and friends living close by who are able to give you a helping hand, then why not consider some professional help. A doula (see page 150) is a woman who offers emotional, mental and physical support to mothers during pregnancy, childbirth and the first weeks after the birth.

WARNING Research suggests that intensive exercise raises the mother's core body temperature and causes vasoconstriction (narrowed blood vessels), which reduces blood flow and thus oxygen supply to the uterus, and a raised foetal heart rate. Limit any strenuous exercise to 15 minutes maximum and make sure the activity is supervised.

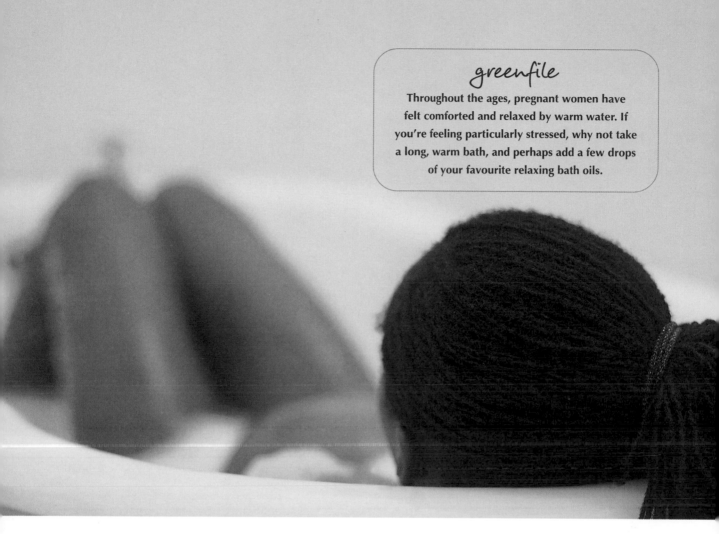

greenfile

Throughout the ages, pregnant women have felt comforted and relaxed by warm water. If you're feeling particularly stressed, why not take a long, warm bath, and perhaps add a few drops of your favourite relaxing bath oils.

Changing Pace

It's very easy to push yourself too hard when you're pregnant. Like most women, you are probably used to juggling 101 different tasks and responsibilities at the same time. If you've always been an active, busy person and/or a hard-working professional, then you're probably used to pushing yourself to get everything done before you collapse at the end of the day. And the odds are that you'll continue this pattern into your pregnancy. Most of the time, we manage to cope with this juggling act, but if you continually over-extend yourself, especially during pregnancy, you will end up burning out.

You must be kind to yourself at this stage in your life. It is important during your pregnancy to listen to your body; to take time to rest or sleep when you feel tired; to stop over-extending yourself. Instead, you need to draw your strength around you in order to stay healthy and to bring a healthy baby into the world. If this means accepting help from others, against all your instincts, then so be it. It is not a sign of weakness. On the contrary, it is a sign that you are listening to your body and to your woman's wisdom.

greenfile

Research shows that laughter creates physiological changes in the body that seem to lower the body's production of stress hormones. So try to see the humour in every situation – a good laugh may be just what you need to stay healthy.

WOMEN'S WISDOM
Women's intuition is legendary, albeit often the butt of men's jokes, but now is a good time to tune in to your own intuitive knowledge. You may instinctively know what's right for you and your baby during pregnancy and labour. You may dream about your baby and feel that you know him before he's born. Your psychic skills may come to the fore and you may be more aware of what's happening to family and loved ones through this sixth sense. Don't be afraid of this women's wisdom. It is there to help you, to allow you to be more comfortable with who you really are and to assist you in tuning in to your body's own language.

Listen to Your Body

We would all benefit from listening to our bodies more closely at all stages of our lives, but pregnancy is the ideal time to start becoming more aware of what's happening in your body, because you are undergoing such dramatic physical and emotional transformations.

This is not merely about growing to accept and hopefully like your new shape. It's about thinking about your self-perception as your social role changes from single woman to mother. It's about tuning in to your heightened physical and emotional sensations.

This is a unique time in your life where you can allow yourself the time to immerse yourself in the language of your body. It is also perhaps the only time when other women are apt to speak about their bodies so openly and, as you share your experiences regarding the physical and emotional changes you are undergoing, so you become more comfortable and confident about listening to your own body and trusting the messages you receive.

Basic Signals

Perhaps the most obvious place to start is by paying attention to the most basic signals that your body will be giving out on a daily basis; namely, hunger, thirst, fatigue and toilet necessities. Sounds pretty rudimentary doesn't it, but how often have you ignored the urge to go to the lavatory, rather waiting for a more convenient time or putting it off until you can't wait any longer? In fact, if you do this repeatedly, you are in danger of getting a urinary tract infection, which is common during pregnancy.

Similarly, do you eat when you are hungry, or do you wait until the prescribed mealtimes? Worse still, do you try to curb your appetite because you fear putting on too much weight while pregnant? Listening to your body is so important at this time, and especially regarding food.

Signals that you are hungry should be obeyed. That's not an excuse to snack on sweets and biscuits. However, your body may require several smaller meals or snacks that are easier to digest rather than eating three large meals a day.

Some signals need to be heard and interpreted. For example, if you have a craving for something sweet, your body may need more energy. Don't be tempted to ignore your body's signals and to override your feelings of fatigue by taking in coffee, chocolate or sugar. That is a short-term and short-sighted solution. You'd be better recognizing your body's message that you need more energy and taking in some complex carbohydrates, such as nuts, cereal bars or crackers with cheese, or eating protein-rich snacks, such as hard cheese or a pot of low-fat yoghurt. Combining the two (a yoghurt with cereal or nuts), will provide you with more lasting energy.

Signals that you may interpret as feeling a bit miserable or under the weather, such as feeling weepy, faint, irritable, cold or clammy and headachey, could in fact mean that your blood sugar levels are too low and you need a square meal.

You'll soon find that your intuition rarely, if ever, lets you down. The more you recognize and respond to your body's signals, the better you will feel.

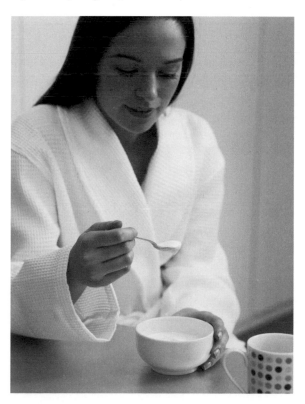

Your Sex Life

It's a pretty sure bet that if you experience nausea in the first few months of your pregnancy, then you are not going to feel like a rampant sex life. However, morning sickness notwithstanding, there is no reason why you should not enjoy a healthy sex life throughout your pregnancy.

Pregnancy is a nine-month continuum and there may be times when you will feel sexy and other times when you won't but rest assured that it is perfectly safe to make love throughout the nine months – research does not show any increased risk of miscarriage from having sex.

Yet another common worry – especially among men – is that sex during pregnancy might hurt the baby. However, the amniotic fluid that surrounds the baby is there to protect and cushion against external bumps and bashes, so the baby cannot be harmed when you make love. In the extremely rare event that your baby is at risk due to you having a low-lying placenta, for example, your doctor or midwife should detect this and give you the relevant advice.

Although there may be times when you lose interest in sex, particularly in the first and last weeks, making love can be particularly enjoyable during pregnancy. You become aroused more easily as a result of the increase in hormone levels and the spontaneity of no contraceptive concerns.

As you get larger, however, you may need to revise the positions you use in love-making. If the bump gets in the way of the traditional man-on-top position, try sitting astride his lap, kneeling with him behind or lying side by side like spoons. This position is particularly effective in later pregnancy because your weight is supported.

greenfile

If your baby is overdue, many women swear that having sex can induce labour, although there is no scientific evidence to support this claim.

Emotional Support

Even the most longed-for pregnancy brings with it concerns, stresses and pressures for both parents. So this is a time when, as a couple, you need to re-evaluate your needs and expectations regarding emotional support.

Irrespective of whether or not you are enjoying an active sex life, it is important that you discuss how you feel emotionally and sexually as openly as possible and from the heart. Each partner needs to listen to and nurture the other's emotional needs and expectations, but you must also feel free to express how you feel in response.

Sometimes, if a pregnant woman is less interested in intimacy, her partner can feel rejected. By the same token, if she perceives that her partner finds her growing and changing body unattractive, this can be extremely hurtful. These sexual tensions need to be discussed between you before they grow out of all proportion.

Of course, if your sexual needs differ at this time, there are other alternatives that can sustain intimacy and a loving relationship. Cuddling, stroking and massage are all alternatives to sexual intercourse that can keep a committed, loving relationship on an even keel.

A final, gentle word of warning: many pregnant women fall into the trap of expecting their partner to anticipate their new needs during pregnancy, whether these are physical, emotional and/or sexual. However, your partner cannot read your mind, so you must share your expectations and desires with him so that he can respond, hopefully empathetically and lovingly.

Post-baby Sex

Without wishing to get ahead of ourselves, it's worth giving a little thought in advance to resuming your sex life after the baby is born, as you can become pregnant again very soon after the birth. As to when it's safe to resume your sex life, this is entirely down to personal circumstances and preferences. You should not have sex if you are still discharging – and most women don't want to have sex at this time anyway – but otherwise, you can have sex as soon as you both feel ready. Your midwife, health visitor or doctor will be happy to discuss contraception choices with you.

cap check

If you used a diaphragm or cap before you became pregnant, check with your doctor or family-planning clinic to make sure it still fits after the birth of your baby since your vagina and cervix change shape during pregnancy and birth. If you later lose or gain more than 3 kg (7 lb), get the fitting checked again.

greenfile

Breast-feeding can act as a very effective contraceptive only if you are fully breast-feeding a baby under six months, i.e. you must be breast-feeding at regular intervals, day and night; giving your baby no other food or drink, so no breast-feeds are missed, and have no periods. Research shows that there is a 1–2 per cent failure rate with fully breast-feeding, which is comparable to condoms. But you have to follow the rules. If you don't want to take any risk whatsoever, then use contraception.

Relaxation Techniques

Pregnancy is a time of unknowns and uncertainties. Women who have been in control of their lives can be disconcerted by the feeling that the events of pregnancy are unfolding beyond their control. Add in the cocktail of hormones coursing through the body, which can cause a bewildering spectrum of emotions in quick succession, and you can see why some women find pregnancy stressful.

Yoga

Yoga is ideal for expectant women and new mothers as it strengthens, tones and relaxes the body and mind. It is also excellent for opening up the pelvis before the birth.

One of the most popular forms of yoga in the West is hatha yoga, which uses postures (asanas) and breathing techniques (pranayamas) to help you to become calm and relaxed. There are other forms of yoga; some more esoteric forms concentrate on the body's energy centres (chakras) and the flow of life energy (prana) through the physical and non-physical or 'subtle' bodies, often incorporating meditation and visualization into the practice.

> **WARNING After 30 weeks, you should not attempt the yoga positions that are performed on your back.**

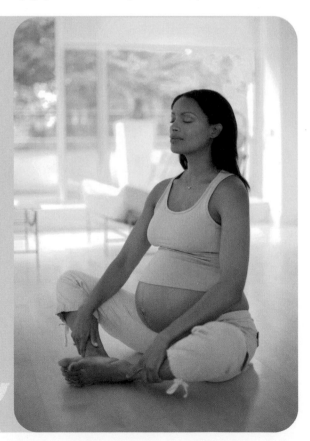

COBBLER'S OR TAILOR'S POSE (*BADDHA KONASANA*)

The following pose is excellent for opening the hips and pelvis in readiness for the birth.

Sit with your back straight and legs outstretched in front of you.

Bend the knees, bringing the soles of your feet together and letting your knees fall out to either side.

Keep your spine long, and press the outer edges of the feet together strongly.

Don't force the knees down or bounce them, rather let them fall until they reach a comfortable level. With practice, they will go further.

Tip: If it helps, you can put some padding under your seat bones, and position a block under each knee for support, if necessary.

Whichever form of yoga you choose, it can be highly beneficial for aiding relaxation, and alleviating various pregnancy ailments, such as backache, joint pain, depression and respiratory problems.

It is recommended that you find a class that is specifically designed for pregnant women, or at the very least, make sure that your teacher is aware of your situation so she can suggest positions that are comfortable and appropriate for pregnancy.

Some teachers recommend that you avoid using yoga in the first trimester of your pregnancy. You should never practise yoga if you are in pain or unwell, and stop if any position becomes uncomfortable.

Meditation and Visualization

You can deepen your state of relaxation by using meditative and relaxation techniques. There are various recognized forms of meditation but most rely on the principle of emptying your mind of clutter and focusing on a specific thought or image, such as a flower or candle. Sometimes a word or mantra is repeated to help focus the mind.

Research shows that during meditation, the brain produces alpha brainwaves, provoking a state of deep relaxation, lowering blood pressure and decreasing muscle tension.

There are numerous meditation CDs or DVDs available to guide you through the process or you could consult a practitioner.

Visualization is a similar technique to meditation but rather than focusing on a single thought or image, you picture a positive scenario or outcome for a situation that is worrying you. For example, you might visualize a swift and straightforward birth, or you

CONNECTING WITH YOUR BABY

The following visualization exercise is designed to help you connect with your unborn baby:

Sit in a comfortable, quiet place where you won't be interrupted.

Slow your breathing until it becomes rhythmic and steady: breathe in through the nose and out through the mouth.

Place your hands on either side of your 'bump'.

Focus on your breath, and visualize it spreading from your lungs, through your bloodstream and into your baby, energizing him.

As you exhale, see the air leaving your body, taking stress and anxiety with it as you blow out.

Continue for as long as is comfortable. When you are ready to stop, slowly open your eyes and bring your consciousness back to the room.

As your breathing returns to normal, so you can resume your normal activities.

NOTE As your energized breath reaches your baby, he may respond to it by wriggling or turning inside the womb.

might picture your unborn child and think about the positive future you will have together. Alternatively, you may choose to imagine a calming scene, such as a palm-fringed beach or a flower-strewn mountainside, to relieve stress.

WARNING Meditation and visualization are powerful tools for relaxation. However, if you are at all concerned about the techniques involved, or if you experience disturbing images at all, then please consult a qualified practitioner or your GP.

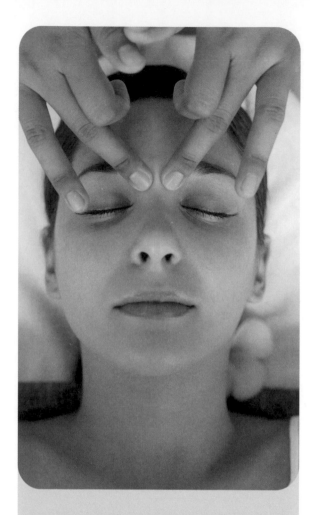

Massage

Throughout history and still in some traditional societies today, pregnant women are regularly given massage by their midwives and care givers. It is believed that massaging the body, especially the tummy, hips and legs, allows the mother to relax but also to become comfortable with and aware of her changing shape.

Massage also gives traditional midwives the opportunity to check routinely on the baby's position and, towards the latter stages of pregnancy, to massage the baby into the correct position if necessary.

In the developed world, sadly, massage is not an integral part of antenatal care but it is still hugely beneficial. A full massage has a similar effect to doing exercise: it stimulates blood flow, which in turn oxygenates the mother's and baby's body. This helps to reduce fatigue, listlessness, nausea and even mild depression.

A regular massage, provided either by your partner, a friend or a professional massage therapist, will help you to relax deeply and it can be especially helpful to those experiencing sleep problems during pregnancy. Massage can also help to relieve general pregnancy problems ranging from aches and pains to backache and headache.

It doesn't matter that your partner may not be formally trained in massage. A simple back or belly rub or a foot massage each night is great for keeping intimacy alive, especially if you are not keen on sex at this time. It also gives your partner a chance to feel close to the growing baby, as well as releasing tension for you.

If you don't have anyone whom you trust to give you a massage, all is not lost. You can always enjoy the same benefits by giving yourself a massage (see right), although you cannot effectively massage the upper back this way. Nonetheless, this is a great way to relax yourself, to ease aches and pains and to communicate with your baby.

AROMATHERAPY OILS TO AVOID DURING PREGNANCY

If massaging directly on to the skin, it is safe to use carrier oil. Seek advice if you wish to add a few drops of aromatherapy oils.

However, the following oils should be avoided during pregnancy:

aniseed, arnica, basil, clary sage, cypress, fennel, jasmine, juniper, marjoram, rosemary

WARNING Massage is usually safe for most pregnant women, although it is advisable to check with your doctor prior to having one. If you have high blood pressure or diabetes, prenatal massage is not recommended.

1 Begin the massage by sitting comfortably on the floor in a warm room. You can be clothed or you may prefer to use a pure carrier oil, such as sunflower, sweet almond or grapeseed oil, to rub directly on to your naked skin.

2 Place the palm of both hands on your stomach and, using light circular movements, gently massage the whole area. Use only as much pressure as is comfortable and don't forget to breathe naturally.

3 After several minutes, bring your hands behind your back with your thumbs facing down towards your abdomen and fingers resting on your lower back. With the flats of your fingers, make light circular strokes all over your lower back. Stretch only as far as you can comfortably reach – this will vary as the pregnancy progresses.

4 Using the flat or the back of your hands, rub up and down or use the fingertips to ease areas of tension in your lower back.

5 Finally, stroke up from your buttocks to your waist in an alternate hand stroking movement.

6 Now, lie down and rest with your hands, palms facing down, just below your navel. As your bump gets bigger you may be more comfortable lying on your side. Don't forget to talk to your baby as you massage. You may like to play some soothing music in the background and dim the lights for complete relaxation.

Miscarriage

Sadly, more than one in five pregnancies in Britain end in a miscarriage. Yet most miscarriages happen before the twelfth week and are relatively rare after that period. Still, a miscarriage can be potentially devastating for both parents, however early it occurs.

The cause of these miscarriages is rarely known but rest assured it is extremely unlikely to be anything you have done or not done. Whether you stayed in bed from the day of your positive pregnancy test or spent every day mountain biking, it wouldn't change things. It's nature's way of making sure that when you do have a baby, it has the best chance for all of its life.

If a miscarriage should unfortunately happen to you, it is important that you and your partner are able to address your feelings of loss, and if necessary allow yourselves a period of bereavement.

Although it may be painful to discuss, it can be extremely valuable to talk about your loss to your midwife, health visitor or family doctor, or contact the Miscarriage Association (see Useful Contacts, page 156). Professional counselling may also be helpful and advisable in some cases. Single mothers, in particular, may well benefit from additional emotional support.

Support for Fathers

Since it is the woman who goes through the physical process of miscarriage and undergoes any medical intervention (she may need an operation or medical treatment to empty her womb), the focus of attention tends to fall on her.

Yet the father can be just as devastated – both mentally and emotionally – so try to ensure that you both seek support.

It is also common for the man to feel the need 'to be strong' for you, and consequently not show how badly he is hurting, which may appear as being uncaring. So try to be honest with each other and share your feelings.

Remembering Your Baby

Although the risk of miscarriage decreases dramatically after 12 weeks of pregnancy, rarely it can still happen up to week 24 (after which time it is known as a stillbirth). In the case of a late miscarriage, many parents benefit from being helped to remember their baby in some way, and over the last decade many hospitals have developed more sensitive procedures for dealing with these issues.

The following provisions are offered by some hospitals. In later miscarriages, some hospitals will take a photograph of the baby for you. Others may offer a hand- or footprint. You may be able to arrange for the hospital chaplain or a representative from your own faith to give a short service, prayer or blessing for your baby. Some hospitals arrange regular services of remembrance or have a Garden or Book of Remembrance in which your baby's details can be entered.

There's no ruling for what happens to your baby's body if you deliver before 24 weeks (unless there are signs of life), but hospitals may offer cremation or burial. If parents want a burial or cremation, or want to take away fetal remains to dispose of themselves (in accordance with environmental regulations), they should discuss this with the hospital. For more information and a booklet discussing the options available, contact the Royal College of Nursing (see Useful Contacts, page 156).

Recovery Time

After the miscarriage, a D&C (dilation and curettage) or evacuation is carried out to reduce the chance of infection and ensure that you don't continue bleeding over the following weeks. The D&C doesn't weaken your cervix or make you more likely to miscarry in subsequent pregnancies.

You may bleed for up to two weeks, and possibly experience cramping pains. If the pain is severe or the blood loss very heavy, contact your doctor without delay. It's advisable to use pads rather than tampons and to refrain from sex until the bleeding has stopped, to avoid the risk of infection. You should get your next period in four to six weeks after the miscarriage.

POSSIBLE CAUSES OF MISCARRIAGE

AGE There is a rise in miscarriage risk as maternal age increases. For women under 35, the clinical miscarriage rate is 6.4 per cent, for age 35–40 it is 14.7 per cent and over the age of 40 it is 23.1 per cent.

GENETIC ABNORMALITY About half of all early miscarriages occur because of chance chromosome abnormalities.

WEIGHT It is important to fall within the recommended weight band for your height. Being either under- or overweight can lead to an increased risk of miscarriage.

ENVIRONMENTAL HAZARDS There is a 30–50 per cent increased risk of miscarriage in women who smoke. Also, both smoking and drinking can adversely affect the quality of a man's sperm. This in turn can lead to a genetic abnormality if such sperm fertilize an egg and so the pregnancy miscarries.

INFECTIONS A high temperature and some specific illnesses or infections, such as German measles (rubella), may cause miscarriage.

ANATOMICAL PROBLEMS If the cervix (neck of the womb) is weak, it may start to open as the uterus becomes heavier in later pregnancy and this can lead to miscarriage.

TESTS Chorionic Villus Sampling (CVS) and Amniocentesis, which are tests offered during some pregnancies, carry a 1–3 in 200 chance of miscarriage (see page 97).

RADIATION The jury is still out on whether or not radiation from VDUs can cause miscarriage, but enough concerns have been raised for you at least to limit the time you spend at the screen or to use a screen protector, if possible (see page 68).

How quickly you return to normal activities depends on the individual. You can expect to feel physically low for a week or so and you should try to take things easy during this time. Do not attempt to return to work until you feel physically and emotionally strong, unless you find the routine, the support and sympathy of colleagues and the focus of work helpful.

Doctors' opinions vary on how long you should wait before trying for another baby, but most advise that you wait until you've had at least one period. More importantly, you must feel physically and emotionally ready to try again. If you are not ready to conceive immediately, do review your choice of contraception, since you can ovulate during the first weeks following your miscarriage.

Fears for the Future

After a miscarriage it is perfectly natural to worry about whether you will ever have a healthy baby but the prospects of a successful pregnancy are better than you think; even people who have had three miscarriages still have a 60 per cent chance of having a successful pregnancy next time, although this figure varies with age. In fact, medical investigations are rarely instigated until after at least three miscarriages. When you conceive again, try to take the next pregnancy one day at a time and to share your feelings and fears with your partner, friends, GP or midwife if it helps.

Homeopathy can be used to great effect in regard to miscarriage, not only to help with physical symptoms but also to address grief issues (see page 114).

greenfile

Some pregnant women are afraid that if they should have a fall or over-exert themselves physically, they may miscarry, but these are not generally causes for concern. The baby is well cushioned inside the womb and should be perfectly safe. However, if you do a lot of high-impact activities, such as horse riding, running or aerobics, you may like to consider a lower impact alternative until after the birth.

Healthy Eating

Eating healthily and getting the best nutrition for you and your unborn baby is important no matter at what stage of pregnancy you are. Yet there is so much conflicting advice and so many old wives' tales about what constitutes good nutrition during pregnancy that it's easy to become confused and anxious about what you should or should not be eating.

Undoubtedly, a good balanced diet throughout your pregnancy will ensure that your baby develops as naturally and healthily as possible and, ideally, you should start looking at your diet before you try to conceive so that you are in prime condition for the pregnancy and birth. But, if it's not a planned pregnancy, it's never too late to start with proper nutrition.

In this chapter, we look at the pregnancy superfoods (see page 44) that will give your unborn baby the best boost for optimum growth and development, and those foods and substances that you should really try to avoid (see page 50), at least for the nine months of your pregnancy.

If you follow a special diet, we will explore how best you can make that diet work for you and your baby (see page 54). We'll also look at how to deal with the thorny issues of cravings (see page 60) and weight gain in the most natural way possible.

The old adage 'you are what you eat' is definitely true and never more apt than during pregnancy. So, to maximize your baby's opportunity to develop healthily in the womb and to avoid disease later in life, a natural and healthy diet – plus a little of what you fancy – is the way forward.

Pregnancy Superfoods

Although the overriding principle of good nutrition during pregnancy is to enjoy your food and to be realistic about what you can change in your diet in order to eat more healthily, there are certain key elements of your diet that are essential if you are to nurture a healthy pregnancy for you and your baby.

Midwives and other health professionals place the greatest emphasis on a handful of 'superfoods', and the general consensus is that while you do not need a special diet when pregnant, you should definitely include the following high-nutrient powerfoods in your daily meal planning.

Spinach

Together with broccoli and other dark green leafy vegetables, spinach is the heavyweight of superfoods for pregnant women. That's because it is rich in folic acid, also known as folate or folacin, which is one of the B group of vitamins, which is essential for your developing baby's health (see page 23).

While it is recommended that before you conceive and during the first three months of pregnancy, you take a daily folic acid supplement (see page 58), you should also make sure you include lots of folate-rich foods in your diet, too (see list, above right). Folic acid in foods is easily destroyed by overcooking, so wherever possible, either lightly steam folate-rich vegetables or eat them raw.

Other good food sources of folates:

Leafy green vegetables, including salad leaves	Bran flakes
	Wheatgerm
Brussels sprouts	Tinned salmon
Jacket potato	Hard-boiled egg
Asparagus	Papaya
Broccoli	Orange
Black-eyed beans	

Watercress

Packed full of iron, this is a true pregnancy superfood. During your pregnancy, your body makes so much extra blood that your iron requirements are much greater than at any other stage in life. Iron helps red blood cells transport oxygen to all parts of the body. However, your growing foetus is also building up its own iron reserves by taking the iron from your body. If your stores of body iron become depleted, you may feel tired and lacking in energy, and you may become anaemic, so make sure you get plenty of these iron-rich foods in your diet.

greenfile

Thanks to Popeye, spinach is probably the most well-known source of iron from our diet. Paradoxically though, spinach contains a substance that makes it hard for the body to absorb its iron, so you're better choosing other sources if it's iron that you're after.

VITAMIN C PLUS IRON
To help your body absorb more of the iron from your diet, try combining food or drinks rich in vitamin C, such as oranges, orange juice, strawberries, kiwi fruit, peppers and tomatoes, with foods rich in iron from non-meat sources.

WARNING Although liver is a good source of iron, if you're pregnant you should avoid eating it because of the amount of vitamin A it contains (see page 51).

Other good food sources of iron:

Meat, especially red meats

Beans and pulses

Nuts, such as cashews, coconut, almonds, hazelnuts, pine nuts, macadamias and pistachios

Dried fruit, especially dried apricots

Wholegrains, such as brown rice, wholemeal pasta and bread

Fortified breakfast cereals

Soybean flour

Most dark green leafy vegetables (such as watercress and curly kale)

Brazil Nuts

A handful of Brazil nuts each day will provide you with a good supply of zinc and selenium. During pregnancy, your body needs zinc to produce and repair DNA, the body's genetic map and basic building blocks of cells, at a time when rapid cell growth is occurring.

Other good food sources of zinc:

Fortified breakfast cereals

Baked beans

Red meat and poultry

Nuts

Wholegrains

Dairy products

Yoghurt

Eating yoghurt is a great way to give your calcium stores a boost, particularly if you're not keen on milk. Calcium has a number of important functions for pregnant women. Its superfood credentials include helping to build strong bones and teeth, regulating

Although oysters are the richest food source of zinc, experts caution against eating raw oysters during pregnancy because of the risk of food-borne illness.

greenfile

You need vitamin D, a fat-soluble vitamin, to aid absorption of calcium in the body during pregnancy. Vitamin D is found in milk and oily fish, so try to include these in your diet alongside foods rich in calcium.

muscle contraction, including the heartbeat, making sure blood clots normally.

Other good food sources of calcium:

Milk

Cheese and other dairy foods

Green leafy vegetables (such as broccoli, cabbage and okra, but not spinach)

Soya beans

Tofu

Soya drinks with added calcium

Nuts, especially almonds and Brazil nuts

Sesame seeds

Bread and anything made with fortified flour

Fish where you eat the bones, such as sardines, tinned salmon and pilchards

Blueberries

A fantastic superfood at any time but especially when pregnant, blueberries are bursting with antioxidants, folates, fibre and oodles of vitamin C, which is essential for your iron absorption and hormone production.

Other good food sources of vitamin C:

Most fruits, especially citrus and kiwi fruits
Berries, including strawberries, blackberries
    and cherries
Potatoes
Parsley

Avocados

Sliced in salads or spooned straight from the skin, this versatile fruit (yes, it is!) is packed full of vitamin E, which promotes new cell development in your baby and may help pregnant women deal with toxins.

Mothers pass vitamin E to their babies in the last 12 weeks of pregnancy (about 20 mg in total), so that is the time to stock up on avocados and other food sources of this important vitamin.

Other good food sources of vitamin E:

Plant oils, such as soya, corn and olive oil, provide the
    richest sources

Nuts	Brussels sprouts
Soya beans	Spinach
Vegetable oil	Wholemeal products
Broccoli	Eggs

> Some very premature babies (born at less than 28 weeks) can show signs of vitamin E deficiency soon after birth if they are born before the transfer from mother to baby takes place.

Sardines

If you believe the hype, foods rich in essential fatty acids (omega-3 and omega-6) are the superfoods to top all superfoods and that's certainly true where pregnancy is concerned. Recent research suggests that pregnant women have increased need of essential fatty acids, because they are important for your baby's neurological growth and brain development.

Other good sources of essential fatty acids:

Plant oils, such as flaxseed, rapeseed, hempseed,
    soybean, cottonseed and blackcurrant seed oil

Tuna	Nuts
Salmon	Seeds
Mackerel	
Herring	

Apricots

These are the perfect pregnancy snack food. Packed full of folate, calcium, magnesium and fibre, they are also a great source of beta-carotene, the plant based form of vitamin A. Beta-carotene helps to strengthen your immune system and that of your developing baby. It's also beneficial for the development of your baby's skin and eyes.

> Choose naturally coloured dried apricots (preferably organic) that have not been treated with sulphur.

Other good food sources of beta-carotene:

Carrots	Greens
Sweet potatoes	Winter squash
Kale	Coriander
Spinach	Thyme

WARNING Extremely high doses of vitamin E have been linked with risks of internal bleeding but, as a fat-soluble vitamin, it is quite hard to overdose.

Baked Beans

It may sound like a joke, but the humble baked bean (as long as it's low sugar) is a great source of vegetable protein, fibre, folate and calcium. In fact, all pulses (beans, lentils and peas) supply the amino acids that the body needs and, as such, are a cheap and nutritious pregnancy superfood that can easily be added to soups, casseroles and curries.

Other good food sources of fibre and vegetable protein:

Chickpeas	Peas
Lentils	Beans

greenfile

Beta-carotene is easily destroyed on cooking, so vegetables containing vitamin A should be lightly steamed or eaten raw to get the optimum nutritional value.

WARNING Retinol, the animal form of vitamin A, can be harmful to unborn babies in large doses, so avoid sources such as cod liver oil. Antenatal supplements contain the plant-derived form of vitamin A (beta-carotene), which is perfectly safe.

Magnesium

Often overlooked as a nutrient, magnesium is in fact classed as a pregnancy superfood because it helps to build and repair your body tissue, and a severe deficiency during pregnancy may lead to pre-eclampsia (high blood pressure and swelling), birth defects and infant mortality.

While calcium stimulates muscles to contract (see Yoghurt, page 45), magnesium stimulates them to relax. In this way, these two 'super' minerals work in tandem. Research suggests that proper levels of magnesium during pregnancy can help keep the uterus from contracting until week 35. Conversely, a magnesium deficiency at this point could lead to premature labour.

You'll get a good natural source of magnesium from green leafy vegetables, wholegrains and wheatgerm, nuts and seeds (such as almonds, pumpkin or sunflower seeds), starches (such as pasta) and milk.

Organic Food

Despite recent assertions by the UK's Consumer Association and Food Standards Agency that organic food produce is neither any safer nor of greater nutritional value than non-organic produce, many holistic practitioners and nutritionists still believe that organic food represents the safest option for pregnant women.

Some experts maintain the levels of chemicals found in conventionally produced foods are perfectly safe, but even low levels of chemicals have been found to be detrimental to the health of a developing foetus and of young children, due to their sensitive, developing immune systems.

Although it is not essential to eat organically grown foods (but good if you can), wherever possible you should try to choose food items that are minimally processed, if at all, and with few or no additives or preservatives.

Top ten pregnancy superfoods

These foods are packed with vitamins, minerals and nutrients. If you
can eat some of these each day, you'll be doing yourself and your
unborn baby a great service.

Bananas, oranges and other fresh fruit

Dried apricots and prunes

Broccoli and other green vegetables

Salmon and other oily fish

Wholemeal bread and brown rice

Lean red meat, chicken and turkey

Yoghurt

Pulses and lentils

Fortified breakfast cereals

Nuts and seeds

Harmful Foods

The general rule of thumb during pregnancy is to eat as you would normally but to try to make sure that you have a balanced diet. For most of us, that means making an effort to eat more fruit and vegetables (five-a-day for optimum nutrition, and preferably organic), plenty of bread, cereals and potatoes together with milk and dairy foods, meat and fish.

However, there are certain foods in a balanced diet that could be detrimental to the health of your unborn child and these should be avoided. The vast majority of 'harmful' foods fall into the category of foods that could cause an infection.

Don't be unduly alarmed, because food infections are in fact rare. However, it is only sensible to take the precaution of avoiding the foods listed below because the effects of food infections (see page 53) can be serious for pregnant women.

Foods to Avoid

Cheese You should avoid eating all types of mould-ripened, soft and blue-veined cheese, such as Brie, Camembert, Stilton or Danish Blue, because of the risk of listeria (see page 53). This is a rare disease that can lead to miscarriage, stillbirth or severe illness in your newborn baby.

Eggs If you eat eggs, make sure they are thoroughly cooked through. Avoid 'runny' eggs or foods containing raw or under-cooked eggs, such as home-made mayonnaise, and certain desserts, such as tiramisu, to prevent the risk of salmonella food poisoning (see page 53).

Meat and poultry Only eat meat and poultry that is thoroughly cooked through without any traces of pink flesh or blood, and wash all surfaces and utensils after preparing raw meat. This will help to avoid infection from toxoplasma (see page 53).

Unpasteurized dairy products This does not apply to the majority of people, but just in case, make sure you do not drink unpasteurized cow's, goat's or sheep's milk or consume their milk products.

Liver Avoid liver or liver products, such as sausages or paté, as liver can contain high levels of vitamin A, too much of which is harmful to your baby (see right).

Raw shellfish Avoid raw shellfish when you're pregnant because it can sometimes contain harmful bacteria and viruses that could cause food poisoning.

Unwashed produce Try to include more fruit, veg and salads in your diet but wash them well before eating and remove all traces of soil. This could contain toxoplasma, which can put your unborn child at risk.

Unhealthy Choices

Wherever possible, try to cut down on the amount of foods you consume containing fat, salt or sugar. The main culprits are snack foods, such as crisps, processed foods, such as pastries, and fast foods, such as take-away and ready-meals.

Salt Although salt is not restricted during pregnancy, most of us already consume more sodium than we need, so it's worth curtailing your intake. If you have a family history of high blood pressure, you may be at risk of toxaemia (hypertension combined with fluid retention and protein in the urine) while you're pregnant, so discuss safe and healthy sodium levels with your GP or midwife as early in your pregnancy as possible.

Sugar This is not unhealthy when consumed in moderation but it does provide calories without providing any nutrients. If you are concerned about excessive weight gain during pregnancy, you should be careful not to over-indulge your sweet tooth. However, you should avoid low-calorie sugar alternatives, containing artificial sweeteners, such as aspartame and saccharine, because their effects on pregnant and lactating women have not been fully studied and there are some concerns surrounding possible health risks.

Caffeine You should also try to drink less tea, coffee and colas, as these contain caffeine. The research regarding caffeine so far is somewhat contradictory but one US study by the Kaiser Permanente Division of Research in 2008 has linked high caffeine consumption to an increased risk of miscarriage. In America, the National Institutes of Health (NIH) recommend a maximum daily caffeine consumption of 300 mg during pregnancy. If you must drink coffee, try to limit yourself to a maximum of two cups per day. Better yet, you could try decaffeinated coffee and caffeine-free teas and soft drinks, or drink fruit or herbal teas.

VITAMIN A

A normal supply of vitamin A is critical for embryonic development and is a requirement for brain development, particularly in its early stages.

It's actually quite easy to get vitamin A from your diet, since it's widely available in meat, dairy, fish, eggs and fortified cereals in the form of 'preformed vitamin A', as well as in most fruits and vegetables in the form of beta-carotene (a nutrient that is converted to vitamin A by your body as needed).

The trick during pregnancy is not to consume too much of the preformed vitamin A, which in high doses can cause birth defects and liver toxicity, with an increased risk of miscarriage. The US government considers 3,000 mcg RAE (10,000 IU) the maximum amount of preformed vitamin A you should take in from supplements, animal sources and fortified foods each day, but you can still get as much beta-carotene as you want from fruits and vegetables.

So be careful if you take any supplements that your practitioner doesn't recommend, as some over-the-counter brands of multi-vitamins contain excessive amounts of preformed vitamin A.

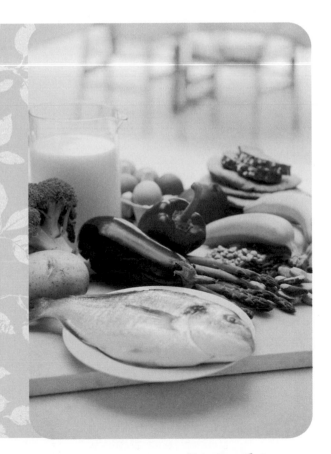

Alcohol

Advice from the Department of Health is that you should not drink alcohol at all if you are pregnant or trying to become pregnant. It is known that if you drink heavily you have an increased risk of miscarriage, and alcohol can cause serious harm to the baby's growth and brain development. Studies show that:

- Pregnant women who drink more than 15 units a week have an increased risk of having a baby with a low birth weight.
- Pregnant women who drink more than 20 units a week have an increased risk of having a baby with some damage to the brain causing impaired intellect.
- Pregnant women who drink very heavily risk having a baby with foetal alcohol syndrome. Babies with this syndrome have brain damage, a low birth weight, and facial malformations.

Since the exact amount of alcohol that is safe during pregnancy is unknown, the safest option is not to drink at all. Your baby is most vulnerable to alcohol during the very early stages of pregnancy, so it is just as important to avoid alcohol when you are trying to become pregnant. If you are going to have an occasional drink during your pregnancy, after the twelfth week is considered to be less of a risk. If you do choose to drink alcohol when you are pregnant, then limit your consumption to one or two units (a unit is half a pint of beer or two-thirds of a small glass of wine, or one small measure of spirits) once or perhaps twice a week. And never get drunk.

If you find it difficult to stop drinking alcohol, then seek advice and help from your practice nurse, midwife or GP.

Women metabolise alcohol more slowly than men do because they tend to have smaller livers and more body fat.

Peanuts

In the past, some nutritionists recommended that you avoid peanuts and food containing peanut products, such as peanut butter and unrefined groundnut oil, during pregnancy if you or the baby's father have a history of asthma, hay fever, eczema or other allergies, in order to reduce the risk of your baby developing a peanut allergy in later life. The official advice from the British government, after extensive investigation of all available studies, is that it is safe to eat peanuts and peanut products during pregnancy (see page 56).

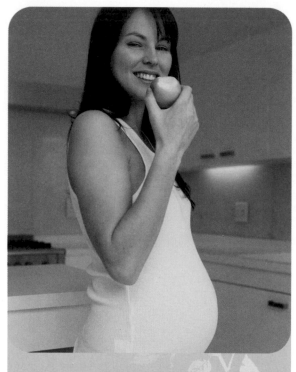

'EATING FOR TWO'
The sad news for foodies is that you can forget the old adage of 'eating for two'. You don't have to increase your food intake during pregnancy – your energy requirements are about 1,940 calories per day, increasing by only 200 calories in the third trimester.

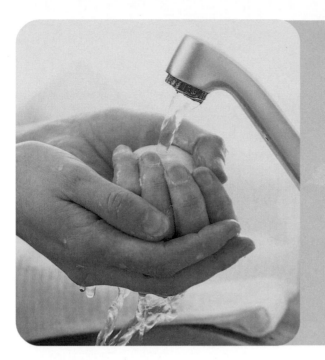

Food Infections

Salmonella This is the most common cause of food poisoning but it does not cross the placenta so, although you may be very unwell, your baby should not be harmed by a salmonella food infection. In exceptionally rare cases, there have been reports of neonatal infection, miscarriage and premature labour.

Toxoplasmosis This is a more serious infection if you are pregnant. It is caused by a parasite picked up by handling or eating raw or undercooked meat or touching infected cat faeces. The infection can cross the placenta and cause miscarriage or deformities. Your baby is at the greatest risk at 10–24 weeks. Treatment for toxoplasmosis during pregnancy is also problematical because the drugs used can adversely affect the foetus.

Listeriosis Perhaps the most serious food infection of them all, listeriosis, resulting from eating soft cheese or undercooked chicken, is thankfully rare (1 in 10,000 pregnancies). If infected, the bacterium can cross the placenta, causing spontaneous abortion in the first trimester of pregnancy and premature labour in the second trimester. As the bacteria can survive in temperatures as low as 4°C (39°F), make sure your fridge is turned down below this level.

greenfile

If you do suffer from a mild gastrointestinal upset from something you've eaten, try sipping a herbal infusion or tea. Aniseed, fennel, mint, ginger or chamomile are all very calming for an upset stomach. See page 120 for home-made ginger tea.

Special Dietary Needs

If you follow a special diet, either as a lifestyle choice or for health reasons, you may be concerned about getting the necessary nutrients for your growing baby. In fact, as long as you pay attention to what you are eating and plan ahead, it is possible to meet all your nutritional needs (and those of your unborn child) while eating many special diets, including vegan, diabetic and macrobiotic.

Indeed, some people believe that a vegetarian diet is healthier during pregnancy, as the foods you eat are less likely to be over-processed or to include so much fat, additives or chemicals.

Nonetheless, you should be aware of certain nutritional pitfalls associated with these diets during pregnancy so that you can make provisions to compensate.

Vegetarian

The primary concern for you as a pregnant vegetarian woman is that you get enough protein and, if you don't eat dairy, calcium too.

Protein can be found in cereals, pulses (beans), nuts, seeds, eggs, soya and Quorn, but protein is not well stored in the body and you need a good supply. To improve your ability to get adequate protein from a vegetarian diet, you should combine sources for optimum effect. So, grains can be combined with smaller amounts of beans or legumes (or dairy products if this applies); and nuts and seeds can be combined with beans or legumes.

greenfile

Ultimately, whichever diet you follow, remember to listen to your body at this time. If you suddenly feel a desire to change or supplement your usual diet during your pregnancy, you should go with the flow. And try to resist the temptation to beat yourself up about breaking your normal dietary rules – after all, these are choices and not written in stone, and you can always revert to your normal code of eating once the baby is born, if you so desire.

Still short of ideas? Well, why not try rice and beans, rice and tahini or macaroni cheese for dinner, while peanut butter on wholemeal toast or a flapjack containing peanuts and sunflower seeds make a protein-packed snack.

Similarly, vegetarians who eat little dairy produce and vegans need to be particularly careful to get enough calcium in the diet. A good intake of calcium-rich foods, such as green leafy vegetables, almonds, sesame seeds or tahini, cow's milk, fortified soya milk, tofu, hard cheese, bread and yoghurt, can

greenfile

Iron absorption is increased if iron-rich foods are eaten with a good source of vitamin C (found in fresh fruit and vegetables). See also page 44.

be improved still further by combining them with vitamin D, which aids calcium absorption. Vitamin D can be obtained from sunlight, margarine, dairy products and some fortified breakfast cereals.

Finally, iron levels normally decrease during pregnancy but vegetarian women are particularly susceptible. Make sure you are getting plenty of iron-rich vegetarian foods, such as wholegrain cereals, pulses, leafy green vegetables, nuts, dried fruits and fortified breakfast cereals.

Don't forget, too, that if you are a vegetarian who relies mainly on pre-prepared or packaged foods, these have still been processed and some of the nutrients of freshly prepared meals will be missing.

If you have any concerns about whether your vegetarian, vegan, macrobiotic or raw-food diet is not providing you with sufficient nutrients, then you should speak to your antenatal healthcare professional, or consult a dietician or nutritionist.

SPECIALIZED DIETS

If you follow any specialized diet while pregnant, it is important that you eat a wide variety of foods to get optimum nutrition, and that you follow the same health advice given to the general population.

VARIATIONS ON VEGETARIAN DIETS

Vegetarian – eats no meat or fish

Lacto-ovo vegetarian – eats no meat but eats dairy products and eggs

Lacto vegetarian – eats dairy but no meat or eggs

Vegan – eats no animal products whatsoever (sometimes including honey)

Macrobiotic – eats wholegrains, beans, vegetables, sea vegetables, seeds and nuts and occasionally fruits in season

Raw food – eats only non-animal foods in a raw state, in particular, fruits, vegetables, fresh juices, sprouts, nuts and seeds

Diabetic Diet

When you become pregnant, the hormones released by the placenta create a resistance to insulin within the body. As a result, it's estimated that between 2–4 per cent of women develop temporary diabetes, known as gestational diabetes. This is normally detected by blood sugar level checks taken between 26 and 30 weeks.

If you have diabetes before pregnancy or develop gestational diabetes, you will receive dietary advice from your health professionals. This will probably include eating regular meals that are lower in fat, reducing the amount of salt in your diet and eating plenty of fruit and vegetables. You will also be encouraged to participate in low-impact activities, such as walking, swimming, yoga and pilates.

Food Intolerance and Allergies

Don't worry about avoiding allergenic foods, such as cow's milk, hen's eggs and nuts, during pregnancy or while breast-feeding as there is no evidence that it will affect your baby's chances of developing an allergy, according to the British Department of Health. In fact, the Department of Health even changed its advice on peanuts in August 2009, saying that you can now eat peanuts during pregnancy with impunity, irrespective of whether you have a family history of food allergies.

However, for high-risk families (those with severely allergic parents or siblings), it's still recommended that pregnant women avoid cigarette smoking and prepare to breast-feed exclusively for at least 4–6 months.

Nonetheless, it has to be said that many women find this advice counter-intuitive. If you prefer to avoid certain known allergens during pregnancy, this cannot harm your unborn child as long as you are eating an otherwise well-balanced, nutritionally sound diet.

greenfile

Since diabetic women have higher levels of blood glucose, which the baby stores as body fat, statistically, they are more likely to give birth to a bigger baby.

GESTATIONAL DIABETES

There is an increased risk of diabetes during pregnancy if:

You are overweight

You smoke or are around smokers more than average

You are over 30

You have a family history of diabetes

You are from certain ethnic minorities

You have a previous history of giving birth to a large baby (more than 4.5 kg or 10 lb)

Reducing Sugar Intake

If you have diabetes or gestational diabetes, or if sugar is detected in your urine, try to cut down on certain foods:

Foods to Avoid

Sugary foods, such as biscuits, cakes, sweet puddings and some tinned foods

Fizzy drinks, cordials and squashes

Fatty or highly processed foods

Salt and salty foods

Foods to Eat Freely

Carbohydrates (bread, pasta, rice, noodles and cereals)

Fruit, vegetables and pulses

Low-fat foods

Supplements

In October 2009, the UK's Royal College of Obstetricians and Gynaecologists (RCOG) released new advice on taking vitamin supplements during pregnancy. Until then, its advice had been in line with the American College of Obstetricians and Gynecologists (ACOG), namely, that if you are a healthy, low-risk-pregnancy woman eating a balanced diet, then routine multi-vitamin supplementation is not necessary.

However, the revised guidance from the RCOG recommends pregnant women should be encouraged to take a multi-vitamin, such as the Healthy Start Vitamin tablet (recommended for pregnancy by the Department of Health/NHS) or another pre-natal multi-vitamin that contains similar doses.

Folic Acid Supplements

The one piece of supplement advice that is agreed upon on both sides of the Atlantic is that when you're pregnant (or if you're trying to conceive), you should take a daily 400 mcg folic acid supplement until the twelfth week of your pregnancy. Folic acid has been shown to reduce the risk of neural tube defects, such as spina bifida. Women are advised to start taking these supplements from the time they stop using contraception because folic acid is particularly important in early pregnancy, but it is never too late to start.

The safety of folic acid was evaluated by the UK's Food Standards Agency's independent Expert Group on Vitamins and Minerals (EVM). The EVM concluded that taking folic acid supplements of up to 1 mg (1,000 mcg) per day is unlikely to do you any harm. Women who are at high risk of having a baby affected by a neural tube defect might be advised by their doctor to take more than 1 mg per day of folic acid. If this affects you, then seek advice from your doctor.

Omega-3

You may have heard that the omega-3 fatty acids contained in fish oil supplements can improve a baby's cognitive development (ability to learn). This may well be the case but there is currently not enough medical evidence to support this claim and more research needs to be carried out before it can be proven. Until then, fish liver oil supplements should be avoided during pregnancy because they contain high levels of vitamin A, which can be harmful to a developing baby (see page 51).

This is not to say that you should not eat fish while you are pregnant. Fish is an excellent source of protein, vitamins and minerals, including omega-3. The Food Standards Agency (FSA) advises that pregnant women who eat a balanced diet do not need to take fish oil supplements because eating a range of fresh fish offers more nutrients than taking supplements alone.

There are non-fish sources of omega-3 fatty acids, such as flax and hemp seeds, but the primary type of

> It is almost impossible for pregnant women to get the full, recommended amount of folic acid from food, which is why the government advises pregnant women to take folic acid supplements.

WARNING If you have diabetes, epilepsy or coeliac disease, you may need to have a higher dose of folic acid. Your doctor or midwife will be able to advise you.

omega-3 fat in these sources is alpha-linolenic acid (ALA). While the body can convert ALA into the more bioactive omega-3 fatty acids called EPA and DHA, the conversion is very inefficient. We get much more benefit from fish oil, which already contain EPA and DHA.

If you are still keen to maximize the effects of omega-3 on your baby's brain development, then what you're really after is a non-fish source for EPA and DHA. Certain algae, such as spirulina (see below), are high in both EPA and DHA and offer your best option for non-fish sourced omega-3.

Vitamin D

The RCOG recommends that women at risk of vitamin D deficiency during pregnancy should take a 10 mcg supplement of vitamin D per day. The at-risk group may include women of South Asian, African, Caribbean or Middle Eastern family origin, those who have limited exposure to sunlight, women who eat a diet that is particularly low in vitamin D and women with pre-pregnancy obesity. If you fall into any of those categories, you should seek advice from your antenatal care team about vitamin D supplementation.

Natural Supplementation

If your diet is healthy and balanced, you may prefer to boost your nutrition by consuming concentrated food sources. For example, spirulina, a blue-green algae, is a useful source of extra protein, especially for vegetarians, and can be taken in powder or tablet form. Molasses is an excellent source of calcium, iron and B vitamins. You can have a tablespoon a day, eaten straight from the jar, or taken in hot water or added to a smoothie. Similarly, liquid chlorophyll is a rich source of iron (take one tablespoon a day).

greenfile

Some women claim that taking vitamin B6 reduces the severity of the nauseous feelings you get from morning sickness, although it doesn't seem to relieve the vomiting.

BANANA AND MOLASSES SMOOTHIE

This delicious smoothie gives you a boost of super-nutritious molasses and it tastes like cappuccino!

5 pitted prunes
1 medium banana, peeled and cut into 2.5-cm (1-in) pieces
2 cups low-fat vanilla soymilk
1 tablespoon blackstrap molasses
¼ teaspoon ground cardamom
3 ice cubes

Place prunes in small bowl and cover with hot tap water. Leave for 15 minutes until plump. Drain. Combine plumped prunes and remaining ingredients in blender and whiz until smooth. If you're feeling decadent, add a scoop of vanilla ice cream.

If you decide to take supplements, choose a specially formulated antenatal, prenatal or pregnancy multi-vitamin to ensure that you do not exceed any of the recommended daily allowances during pregnancy.

Cravings

We've all heard stories of pregnant women who suddenly start to crave certain foodstuffs in the middle of the night, or who can't get enough of some unusual food combinations, such as ice cream and pickled onions. In fact, you've probably heard tell of women who even want to eat peculiar non-food items, such as wallpaper, coal or chalk. Although these fancies during pregnancy undoubtedly happen, the wackier cravings are actually very rare.

In general, food cravings tend to be either for sweet foods or for a favourite childhood dish. In my case, while pregnant with my second child, I had an overwhelming desire to eat mini milk lollies, but thankfully, it lasted only a few days.

No one actually knows for certain what causes food cravings. Many nutritionists suspect that cravings are in response to a temporary deficiency in certain nutrients. Certainly, it is worth using a craving as a timely reminder to take a closer look at what you eat. You may find that due to morning sickness, for example, you're skipping meals and snacking instead, and this means you're missing out on a balanced diet. If your diet is deficient in some way, try to redress the balance or ask your GP, midwife or pharmacist to recommend a suitable vitamin or mineral supplement to take during pregnancy.

If you are craving chocolate each afternoon, it may simply mean that your body needs more energy. Perhaps carrying a snack with you, such as a sandwich, a cereal bar or some fruit, will satisfy your body's craving for energy. If you're still hungry or craving chocolate a short while after eating a more healthy snack, then by all means, have a little of what you fancy.

Other experts believe that cravings are a result of an emotional response to pregnancy – either conscious or subconscious. You may crave a childhood food that is comforting, or perhaps a food that reminds you of your cultural or religious background, especially if you

greenfile

Women suffering from iron deficiency during pregnancy sometimes develop cravings for non-food items, such as clay, dirt, cornflour and ice. If you suddenly find yourself fancying one of these odd items to eat, then get a blood test to check for iron-deficiency anaemia. If you have a low haemoglobin count, you may be prescribed daily iron supplements but you should certainly eat iron-rich foods.

are removed from your family. Cravings can also be ascribed to an unconscious need to honour privately your new special state of pregnancy.

Common Dislikes

In reality, rather than craving particular foods, many women actually find they go off certain foods or drinks, or other tastes. Common dislikes include toothpaste, coffee, tea and alcohol, rich, creamy foods and fried foods. Often, the very smell of these items is enough to make susceptible pregnant women feel quite nauseous, so it's small wonder that this symptom is often related to pregnancy sickness, which some believe is the body's way of making you eat more wisely.

Whether you crave foods or find that you suddenly dislike certain foods, this may be as a result of the fact that your senses of taste and smell are changed in pregnancy. Some women report that these senses are dulled, while others report an odd metallic taste in their mouths in very early pregnancy, which is more pronounced when certain foods are eaten.

Whatever the cause of cravings, and the jury is still out on this one, as long as you are meeting all of your daily needs with a healthy diet, then there is no reason why you should not indulge your desire for the occasional treat.

The danger comes, of course, when your urge to satisfy a craving means that you are drawn to unhealthy items, such as coffee, alcohol or cigarettes, which can harm your baby. Cravings of this nature should be ignored or curtailed. Otherwise, in moderation, enjoy whatever it is that you fancy!

A craving for a non-food item, such as coal, soap or toothpaste, is known as 'pica'. On very rare occasions, pica can be a sign of more serious underlying problems, such as nutritional deficiency or psychological problems.

greenfile
If you crave cheese or ice cream, your body could be telling you that it needs more calcium. In fact, the unusual but not uncommon pregnancy craving of pickles and ice cream is not so hard to understand when you realize that vinegary foods (the pickles) help the body to release calcium (from the ice cream) into the bloodstream – it's nature's way of helping!

One of the most common taste dislikes in early pregnancy is toothpaste. Since commercial toothpastes contain fluoride, foaming agents and other nasty chemicals, you can make your own.

Mix together 1 tablespoon bicarbonate of soda, a pinch of salt, 1 teaspoon lemon juice and 1 drop of peppermint essential oil, adding enough filtered water to mix the ingredients into a paste. The paste hardens if left open to the air, so store it in an airtight container. The beauty of your own home-made toothpaste is that you can choose any flavour you like – it doesn't have to be peppermint – and that way you are far less likely to have an aversion to cleaning your teeth.

Weight Gain

Weight is such an emotive subject for women in the western world. Many newly pregnant women are fearful of gaining excessive weight during the pregnancy that they will then have problems losing after the baby is born. In recognition of this western obsession with being thin, many antenatal clinics have now ceased to weigh women at every visit but, naturally, many women still weigh themselves at home.

If you decide to keep a record of your weight gain at home, make sure you always use the same scales, and that you always weigh yourself at the same time of day wearing just underwear, or similar clothing, each time.

Officially, the expected weight gain during pregnancy for a woman who is the appropriate weight for her height is between 11–16 kg (24–35 lb). However, if you are under-weight at the start of your pregnancy, you could gain as much as 22¾ kg (50 lb) without cause for concern, although somewhere in the region of 12¾–18 kg (28–40 lb) is more common for thinner women. Conversely, if you are overweight when you conceive, you may not gain as much as the average expectation, but you should gain at least 6¾ kg (15 lb). A weight-gain range of 7–11 kg (15–25 lb) is anticipated if you are overweight.

It is unlikely that you will gain weight at a steady rate throughout the pregnancy – you tend to gain in fits and starts. Each woman's weight-gain pattern is unique to her. However, as a general rule of thumb, you can expect to gain moderately in the first trimester and at the beginning of the second trimester, say around 3–4 kg (6–9 lb) in the first 20 weeks. Thereafter, the rate of gain is faster – about 450 g (1 lb) per week on average.

By week 32–33, you will be gaining weight faster than at any other time in your pregnancy. By week 37, your weight gain will probably be slowing down.

greenfile

It is a myth that smaller babies are easier to deliver. Studies show an undernourished mother is more likely to deliver a baby who is also undernourished, and nutritionally deprived babies (low birth weight infants) have a higher risk of newborn complications and delayed growth and development. So, don't compromise your baby by trying to keep weight gain to a minimum.

What is more important than how much weight you gain is the rate of growth of your baby, and this is routinely monitored during antenatal care. You may find that your baby is growing rapidly in the later weeks of the pregnancy but that your weight gain actually slows down. As long as your baby is growing healthily, your emphasis should be on eating nutritiously and enjoying your food rather than how much weight you are putting on. You should try to consume about 2,000 calories of nutrient-rich foods a day, limiting calories from saturated fats and sugars.

Positive Body Image

Concerns about weight gain are often connected to how you view the pregnant form. If you think of yourself as a beached whale and unattractive while pregnant, you will probably consider any weight gain negatively. On the other hand, if you can view your body changes as beautiful and as a blessing, then you are more likely to have a positive approach to your new appearance and to the inevitable increase in your weight.

Even if you are unable to shake off a negative view of your pregnant body image, it is important that you don't consciously or unconsciously cut back on your food intake in an effort to keep your weight gain during pregnancy to a minimum. This is not a safe or sensible plan. Nor should you exercise excessively during pregnancy, particularly if the goal is minimizing weight gain.

Be reassured that most women are able to lose any excess weight after the birth of their baby through exercise and sensible eating. So don't be tempted to compromise a healthy pregnancy by dieting or excessive exercising.

Also, keep in mind that weight charts for expectant mothers, rather like those for growing babies, present ranges and averages. It doesn't mean you are unhealthy if you don't fit the right slot on the chart. However, if you are concerned at all by how much or how little weight you are putting on, speak to your antenatal care team.

BREAKDOWN OF AVERAGE PREGNANCY WEIGHT GAIN

Baby – 3.4 kg (7½ lb)
Enlargement of uterus – 1 kg (2 lb)
Placenta – 750 g (1½ lb)
Amniotic fluid – 1 kg (2 lb)
Breast enlargement – 1 kg (2 lb)
Extra blood and fluid volume – 3.6 kg (8 lb)
Extra fat stores – 3 kg (7 lb)
Total – approx. 14 kg (30 lb)

If you are expecting twins, you can expect to gain an additional 4.5 kg (10 lb) over and above the average weight-gain guidelines.

Healthy Living

The places where you live and work exert an unseen yet powerful influence on your life, both physically and emotionally. Most of the time, you give little thought to your living and working environment, but when you are pregnant, you are far more conscious about your surroundings and the effect they might have on you and your developing baby.

That's why this chapter draws your attention to the dangers that you might be exposed to in your home, especially when cleaning (see page 70), and there's advice on how to make the home and office environments safer, healthier and greener (see page 75).

We also look at the environmental irritants, pollutants and allergens that you may be exposed to, often through a busy social life, without necessarily realizing the risks these might pose. Certainly, when you read about the insidious dangers of second-hand smoke and over-the-counter medicines, you will understand the need for circumspection.

On a lighter note, this chapter will help you to indulge your natural 'nesting' instinct with suggestions for a greener nursery (see page 76) and tips on how to choose the most attractive yet environmentally friendly and natural maternity wear and toiletries (see page 80).

Coping with Work

Unless you work in a hazardous environment or your work is physically strenuous, there is no reason why you shouldn't continue working throughout your pregnancy until around 34 weeks, and a few women elect to work until their due date.

Nonetheless, there may be adjustments that you want to make to your normal work practices and working style for the sake of your health and general well-being.

Commuting

Commuting by bus or train shouldn't pose any particular problems, although you might like to consider changing your working hours to avoid the worst of the rush-hour crush.

In the early stages of your pregnancy, morning sickness can make the early morning commute tricky. Try carrying ginger biscuits, crackers or a snack with you, or practise breathing exercises to alleviate the symptoms. If a bout of nausea persists, don't be afraid to get off the bus or train and wait until the nausea passes before re-boarding – better to be late for work than ill on public transport.

If you drive to work, try to avoid sitting in heavy traffic and always close your car windows when going through a tunnel or in stationary traffic to avoid the build up of fumes.

Even though it can be uncomfortable in the later stages of pregnancy, you should always wear a seatbelt in the car, whether you're driving or a passenger. The American Congress of Obstetricians and Gynaecologists (ACOG) reports that research of crashes and safety belt use in pregnant women suggests that about four out of five babies would have been saved if their mothers had worn safety belts.

DRIVE SAFE

For your safety and comfort, follow these rules when wearing your safety belt:

Always wear both the lap and shoulder belt.

Buckle the lap belt low on your hip bones, below your belly.

Place the shoulder belt off to the side of your belly and across the centre of your chest (between your breasts). The upper part should cross your shoulder without chafing your neck.

Never place the shoulder belt under your arm, off your shoulder or behind your back.

Make sure the belt fits snugly – belts worn too loosely or too high on the belly can cause broken ribs or injuries to your belly.

REMEMBER, most damage is caused when safety belts are not used at all.

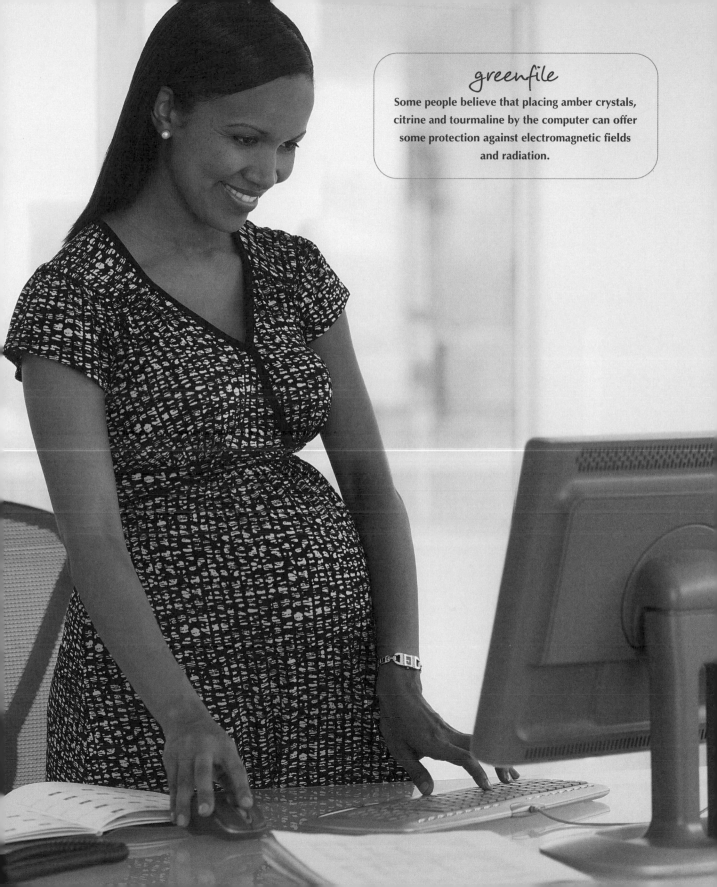

greenfile

Some people believe that placing amber crystals, citrine and tourmaline by the computer can offer some protection against electromagnetic fields and radiation.

Computer Use

There's been speculation since the 1980s that computer monitors (also called video display units, or VDUs) are unsafe for pregnant women because of low levels of radiation (electromagnetic fields). However, in recent years, there have been many research studies into the subject and there is no evidence that computer monitors cause any problems in unborn babies.

That said, this is completely counter-intuitive for many women. In this case, you may prefer to use an anti-radiation, anti-static filter screen on your VDU for additional protection.

What is inarguable is that sitting in front of the computer all day can strain your eyes, cause back pain, and make varicose veins worse. So be sure to take frequent breaks, walk around, and stretch your legs during the day.

Safety and Comfort

As an office worker, there are several precautions you can take to make sure you stay as healthy as possible while working throughout your pregnancy.

Don't be afraid to ask for or to accept help from your colleagues if you need it.

Reduce your exposure to stress at work. If you can't eliminate the stress factor (sadly, a difficult boss doesn't go away simply because you're pregnant), then try to find ways to manage the stress, such as breathing exercises, visualization (see page 37), stretching, or simply taking a break and leaving the building. Physically removing yourself from the source of your stress can, on occasions, work wonders.

Take regular breaks throughout the working day. If you sit for long periods, then stand up and stretch. Conversely, if you've been standing, sit down and rest.

You must nourish yourself. Nutritious snacks and a proper lunch are essential – don't rely on the workplace vending machine to subsist on instant coffee, snacks and biscuits. It's important to stay hydrated, so drink plenty of water.

Keep the circulation flowing in your legs by putting your feet up when you take a break. A box, stool or

WARNING Although working at a computer won't harm your developing baby, pregnant women are more susceptible to carpal tunnel syndrome (numb, achy fingers), so make sure you arrange your desk and chair at the optimum height.

another chair can make a perfectly adequate improvised footstool.

Dress in loose, comfortable clothing and swap your killer heels for a lower heel or flat shoe (see page 80, for more advice on maternity wear).

Put a potted plant on your desk to bring good *yang* energy into your office.

Heavy Labour

You may have a job that requires you to perform considerable amounts of physical labour, which was fine before you were pregnant but could be a strain now. You need to speak to your employer if your job involves:

- repetitive heavy lifting
- pushing or pulling heavy loads
- intense stair climbing
- prolonged standing

It may be possible to find a colleague who can take on some of the more dangerous aspects of your work or you might be offered a temporary reassignment that is less physically demanding.

Alternatively, you may feel that you want to continue in the same post but, in order to minimize the risks to you and your baby from physical exertion, you should take frequent breaks to rest and monitor your physical and emotional stress levels closely.

Working with Chemicals

Should your job involve handling, transporting or exposure to chemicals and pollutants on a daily basis, then you may be best advised to speak to your employer about another temporary position or to stop working altogether, if this is economically feasible. This is because a number of chemicals and pollutants,

in particular lead, mercury, carbon monoxide, pesticides and anaesthetics, have been shown to be particularly dangerous for both your own and your baby's health. Effects of exposure can include:

- premature delivery
- miscarriage
- physical birth defects and deformities
- developmental problems later in life

Of course, it may be that you are unable to make other work arrangements. In which case, if you have to or choose to continue to work with chemicals, you are advised to follow strict safety precautions, namely:

- Wear protective clothing, such as gloves and a ventilator/mask, at all times
- Avoid direct contact with all chemicals
- Remove contaminated or soiled clothing as soon as possible
- Ask your employer for a risk assessment, information on health and safety hazards during pregnancy and to provide additional ventilation equipment

AIR TRAVEL

Most of the time, the fact that your job involves lots of overseas travel is perhaps a huge attraction but it can be a problem when you're pregnant. Many alternative health professionals advise against flying during the first trimester of pregnancy, especially if you have a history of miscarriage. This can be hard to explain if you haven't shared the news of your pregnancy with your boss or colleagues as yet.

If you have to travel by air for work, then you might like to take the flower remedy, yarrow, which can be beneficial but shouldn't be taken in the first trimester. Yarrow essence helps relieve queasiness and feelings of vulnerability, and protects you from absorbing environmental influences that are rife on a plane. There are also special travel sickness blends of flower essences available but check that they are safe for use during pregnancy before buying.

A Clean, Green Home

As you already know, you are more susceptible to pollutants and chemicals when you're pregnant, so as well as eliminating harmful substances from your diet and lifestyle, don't forget about the chemicals that you use everyday around the house.

Many household cleaning products state on the packaging that they may not be safe for inhalation or use by pregnant women. Always read the labels carefully before using any cleaning product.

Since you are already introducing a more natural approach to health and diet into your lifestyle, why not take this opportunity to extend the green principle to keeping house as well?

Cleaning

Certainly, for the duration of your pregnancy, you should avoid the more potent commercial cleaners on the market. Nonetheless, even run-of-the-mill, perfumed proprietary brands can cause headaches, sneezing, sore throats, and irritated eyes, nose and skin.

Your pregnancy is the perfect time to review your household cleaning products and opt for safer, greener alternatives that will ensure a healthier environment to bring your baby home to and in which your child can grow. Cut down on the number of products that you use, and avoid any that carry caution warnings or are corrosive or caustic.

A whole host of safer, milder, eco-friendly cleaners are now available in supermarkets and stores. Based on natural cleansers, these products do actually work. Alternatively, why not use the proven ingredients that past generations used to clean the home? These everyday items are cheap and effective and they pose no health-threat to you or your unborn child.

WARNING Keep all cleaning goods, whether commercial brands or natural products, out of the reach of inquisitive little fingers and mouths. Even natural or safer cleaners can pose a health risk when ingested.

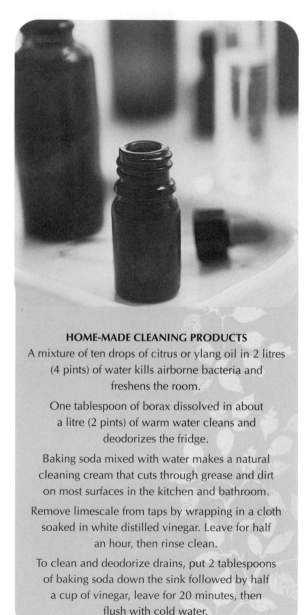

HOME-MADE CLEANING PRODUCTS
A mixture of ten drops of citrus or ylang oil in 2 litres (4 pints) of water kills airborne bacteria and freshens the room.

One tablespoon of borax dissolved in about a litre (2 pints) of warm water cleans and deodorizes the fridge.

Baking soda mixed with water makes a natural cleaning cream that cuts through grease and dirt on most surfaces in the kitchen and bathroom.

Remove limescale from taps by wrapping in a cloth soaked in white distilled vinegar. Leave for half an hour, then rinse clean.

To clean and deodorize drains, put 2 tablespoons of baking soda down the sink followed by half a cup of vinegar, leave for 20 minutes, then flush with cold water.

Natural Disinfectants

Instead of using shop bought disinfectants, try using certain herbal oils and extracts as a natural disinfectant in your home. The anti-fungal and antibacterial properties of oils, such as Australian tea tree oil, pine oil and citrus seed extract, can be put to good use to wipe down nursery surfaces. However, they are not effective against harmful food bacteria, so do not rely on these in the kitchen or dining room.

Green Laundry

Try to reduce the amount of detergent you use in the form of washing liquids and powders, washing-up liquids and dishwasher products. Wherever possible, choose milder alternatives that are kinder to both the environment and your health. You should also opt for unscented, non-biological varieties that reduce the risks of allergic reactions.

You can cut your consumption of detergent powder by substituting baking soda for half the normal dose of commercial powder in each wash. For heavily soiled loads, add half a cup of borax to your usual detergent to boost its power, rather than using stronger detergents.

You can stop using fabric softeners completely since their sole purpose is to coat clothing fibres

greenfile

Furniture polish containing sodium phosphate or turpentine can burn the skin and is dangerous when inhaled, especially during pregnancy. For an easy natural furniture polish, simply place 3 or 4 tea bags (black tea) in a large mug or bowl and pour over boiling water. Allow to steep. When cool, remove the tea bags. Dip a cotton cloth into the tea and wipe over your wooden furniture. You don't even need to rinse. You'll be left with a lovely, natural sheen to your furniture.

greenfile

When replacing a washing machine or dishwasher, check out the eco-friendliness of your new appliance. Whenever possible, choose the greenest machine available at the right price.

temporarily to prevent static cling: since your pregnancy clothes are probably made of natural fibres, such as cotton, wool or linen, fabric conditioners are not necessary. If you still feel the need for fabric softeners, try adding one cup of white distilled vinegar to the dispenser drawer instead.

Green Fingers

Pesticides, fertilizers and herbicides all pose a health risk. While you are pregnant (and once you have a young family), it is well worth looking into the possibility of using organic and traditional gardening methods and integrated pest management. Both options are kinder to our environment and to you and your family.

Suggestions for a natural alternative to gardening pollutants include companion planting (plant three basil plants near a tomato plant to deter white fly and mosquitoes), introducing pest-eating wildlife (a ladybird can eat more than 5,000 aphids per year), and natural barriers (slugs and snails dislike slithering over gritty surfaces so surround precious plants with a thick sprinkling of crushed egg shells, pine needles, coffee grouts or wood ash), as well as the commercial option of buying organic or chemical-free gardening products.

Air fresheners containing carbolic acid or formaldehyde can cause nausea. Use natural essential oils as air fresheners or freshly cut scented flowers, such as stocks.

WARNING Commercial toilet cleaners contain cresol, which is easily absorbed through the skin and can damage major organs. Instead, pour a quarter of a cup of borax around your toilet bowl and leave for an hour or overnight. Then flush for a clean, deodorized toilet.

Environmental Pollutants

Your surroundings can exert an unseen and occasionally dangerous influence on your health and that of your unborn baby. You can limit any health risks by organizing your home environment and changing certain lifestyle habits so that you and your baby enjoy the most natural well-being possible.

Smoking

Most research indicates that pregnant women should not smoke. When you smoke, your baby shares chemicals from the smoke you inhale. These chemicals adversely affect your baby's healthy growth and development. For example, carbon monoxide restricts your baby's oxygen supply, causing his heart to beat harder every time you smoke.

Recent studies also show that smoking during pregnancy can damage your baby's airways before he is even born. As a result, your child may develop smaller airways, making him more vulnerable to breathing problems, such as asthma, once he is born and as he grows up.

As well as all the well-documented threats to your health as a smoker, including a heightened risk of cancer, lung disease and heart disease, there is a more immediate and dangerous risk to your health if you smoke when pregnant. Smoking can damage the placenta, leading to pregnancy complications, such as bleeding and placenta abruption (the placenta starts to come away from the uterus), and these complications can be life-threatening for both you and your baby.

> ### STARTLING STATISTICS FOR PREGNANT SMOKERS
> Smokers are more likely to deliver babies prematurely and at a much lower birth weight.
>
> Smokers are five times more likely to develop eclampsia, which is the leading cause of maternal deaths in the UK.
>
> Smokers are at greater risk of miscarriage and stillbirth.

The general consensus is that you should give up smoking for the duration of your pregnancy at the very least. Quitting smoking might feel difficult, especially if you are already under stress, but you're not on your own – a great deal of support is available to you in the form of helplines (see Useful Contacts, page 156) and your GP's surgery. When you see the drastic improvements to your life and health, and you know it is safeguarding your developing baby, it is really motivating.

Recreational Drugs

While you are pregnant or if you are trying for a baby, you should avoid all recreational drug use. **Marijuana** (cannabis) has not been conclusively proven to cause birth defects, but studies into its use during pregnancy have highlighted a link between the drug and growth and development problems, and babies being born with low birth weights. Babies exposed to cannabis while they're in the womb are also more likely to be restless, irritable and jumpy during the first few weeks after being born.

> ## greenfile
> **Acupuncture (see page 108), when used by itself or in conjunction with other therapies, can be extremely beneficial in removing the craving for nicotine and for helping you to give up smoking. The acupuncture can be general or auricular (needles are inserted in specific parts of the ear).**

PASSIVE SMOKING

It is definitely a step in the right direction for you to give up smoking but if you still live or work with a smoker or spend time in a smoky atmosphere, then you and your developing baby are still at grave risk from second-hand smoke.

Second-hand smoke, or Environmental Tobacco Smoke (ETS) as it is sometimes known, comes from the tip of a cigarette and the smoke that is breathed back out by the smoker. Wherever people smoke, there is second-hand smoke in the air, although you might not notice it because it is almost invisible and odourless.

Even if you open a window, second-hand smoke will still be present in a room after two and a half hours, despite the fact that you may not be able to see or smell it. Travelling with a smoker in a car is even worse as all of the smoke is concentrated into a small space.

People that breathe second-hand smoke are at risk of the same diseases as smokers, including cancer and heart disease, because second-hand smoke contains 4,000 toxic chemicals. It is estimated that second-hand smoke causes thousands of deaths each year. And the dangers are far worse for pregnant women because, as we have seen, the toxins from inhaled smoke can cross the placenta and adversely affect your developing baby.

It is also worth thinking ahead: children are particularly affected by second-hand smoke because their bodies are still developing, and around half of all British children are growing up in homes where at least one parent is a smoker.

If cannabis is smoked with tobacco, additionally, the smoke causes the same problems as for cigarette smokers (see above).

Ecstasy According to recent research, taking ecstasy during pregnancy increases the risk of your baby being born with abnormalities. In particular, babies had limb and heart problems, such as club foot and problems with bones and muscles. The drug poses risks at any time, but particularly during the first trimester, when a baby is going through the crucial early stages of development.

Cocaine and opiates are among the most dangerous recreational drugs for pregnant women, causing potentially life-threatening and long-lasting consequences for your baby.

For example, cocaine users are:

- Twice as likely as other women to give birth prematurely and cocaine can cross the placenta and enter the circulation system of your baby
- At increased risk of miscarriage in the early stages of pregnancy
- At increased risk of premature labour during the later stages of pregnancy
- At increased risk of placental abruption with all its inherent dangers

The babies of pregnant cocaine users are:

- At risk of permanent, serious brain damage
- Prone to a range of other abnormalities, including problems with the skull, heart, face, eyes, limbs, genitals and intestines
- At risk of a range of permanent disabilities
- Likely to have a low birth weight

Heroin is another drug that can cause a host of problems for babies. In particular, it is linked with growth difficulties, stillbirth and premature birth. In fact, half of all babies born to women who take heroin regularly arrive early. In addition, heroin can be passed to a baby through breast-milk and babies may be born suffering with withdrawal from heroin, showing symptoms, such as irritability, restlessness, distress and feeding difficulties.

Of course, if you have a recreational drug issue, no one is under-estimating how hard it is to stop its use, but there is help available (see Useful Contacts, page 156) and the dangers to your unborn child of continued drug use are too serious to ignore.

Prescription Medications

As soon as you realize that you are pregnant, you should consult your doctor about the safety of any prescribed medications that you are taking. Some are able to cross the placenta and adversely affect your baby, but don't abruptly stop taking medication without first seeking advice.

Some over-the-counter medications (OTC) can also affect or harm the foetus or baby, so you should consult your pharmacist before taking any OTC medicine. OTC medication labels should be checked because they contain warnings against use during pregnancy and breast-feeding, if applicable.

Certain types of drugs are particularly problematic. They include antihistamines (commonly contained in cough and cold remedies, allergy drugs, motion sickness drugs and sleep aids) and non-steroidal anti-inflammatory drugs (NSAIDs). Examples of non-prescription NSAIDs are aspirin, ibuprofen, brufen, naproxen sodium, diclofenac and ketoprofen, although they may be marketed under a variety of different brand names. NSAIDs should not be used during the last three months of pregnancy unless specified by a doctor,

greenfile

Do not attempt to give up drugs or deal with addiction alone. Get help from a specialist, a support group such as Narcotics Anonymous, and a complementary medical practitioner.

WARNING If your pregnancy is unplanned and you've been taking drugs, you should stop doing so as soon as possible, as the early stages of development in the womb are crucial and your baby may have been exposed to harm.

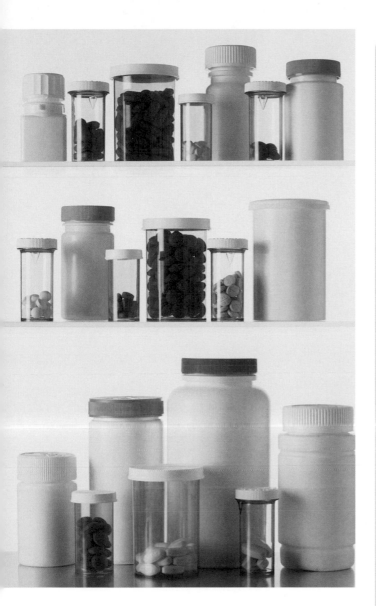

because they may cause problems for your baby or complications during delivery.

As a general rule of thumb, avoid all medication during your pregnancy unless it is specifically prescribed for you. Instead, look at a number of natural alternatives that can help with most of the common ailments (see Chapter 7, Health & Well-being). However, a word of caution: just because something is natural does not mean it's not potent. Take advice before using any herbal or complementary medicines.

REDUCING THE RISK FROM ENVIRONMENTAL POLLUTANTS

Why not take the following precautions to minimize the risk to you and your baby of any environmental pollutants:

Diagnostic X-rays are dangerous for your baby. Wherever possible, postpone unnecessary X-rays or CT scans until after your baby is born. If an X-ray is necessary, tell the doctor or radiologist that you're pregnant, and make sure you're given a protective lead apron to wear.

Don't stand directly in front of a microwave oven while it's in use.

Avoid chemical hazards, such as cleaning agents and garden pesticides (see A Clean, Green Home, page 70).

Radon, a naturally occurring, radioactive gas, can cause cancer. In the USA, the Environmental Protection Agency (EPA) advises pregnant women to contact their local authority or ecological group to establish whether they live in a radon-contaminated area, or buy a radon detector to monitor radon levels in your home.

Avoid using aluminium or copper cookware and don't wrap food in aluminium foil.

Although there is no scientific evidence to suggest that an electric blanket or heating pad can harm your foetus, it is commonly believed that you should avoid sleeping with one on.

The risk of domestic carbon monoxide poisoning caused by leaks from faulty boilers, wood-burning stoves, fireplaces, gas heaters, gas stoves and space heaters can be prevented by early detection with the use of household carbon monoxide detectors and by having these items regularly serviced.

In the United States, you can ask your local environmental safety office to test the lead levels in your drinking water. In the UK, your water company will tell you how likely it is that there are high lead levels in your drinking water. If you are concerned, contact your water company and they should take a sample from your home if necessary, and tell you the results.

Preparing the Nursery

It is a natural instinct, especially in the latter months of your pregnancy, to nest build. Preparing the nursery for your new baby can be a source of such delight but, without wishing to dampen your enthusiasms, it is important that you bear a few safety factors in mind.

When you are pregnant, you and your unborn child are vulnerable to environmental irritants, allergens and toxins so, when assembling your new nursery, you want to take every precaution to protect the both of you.

The good news is that in the past few years a much greater choice of green, environmentally friendly and safe products have emerged in the market with which to decorate and furnish your nursery. They pose far fewer, if any, health risks than synthetic equivalents.

Decorating

You should never sand or repaint your baby's room (or any other room) when pregnant. In old houses, sanding can disturb old lead paint, creating a toxic dust that you then breathe in. It is widely known that lead can cross the placenta, so not only could this dust give you lead poisoning, but it could harm your unborn child as well.

Lead poisoning is such a serious condition that if your partner works with old paint, or takes on the decorating himself, avoid him until he has showered and replaced his work clothes.

If you are concerned about the potential presence of lead, there are commercial companies who will come into your home and test walls, windowsills, doorjambs and house dust. If unacceptable levels are found, or even traces for that matter, the company is equipped and qualified to remove the paint safely. Alternatively, you can get self-test kits from DIY stores to check whether your paintwork contains lead but it will not tell you in what quantity.

If professional removal is not possible, apply a fresh coat of non-toxic paint over the old paint but be careful that it does not start to chip or get repeatedly rubbed, because this could release lead from the old paint layers underneath.

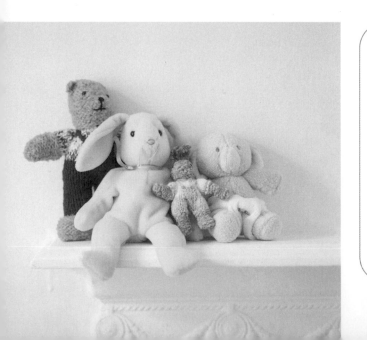

greenfile

Whichever paint you choose, it is important to air the nursery well before your baby is moved into the room. In fact, in Chinese tradition, it is recommended that you air all rooms and replace stale energy once a day by opening windows and encouraging a through draught.

Don't be tempted to use an air freshener to do the job of airing the room. These contain carbolic acid or formaldehyde, which can cause nausea in pregnant women.

Choosing Paint

When choosing a paint or wood finish, check the label for levels of volatile organic compounds (VOCs), which readily vaporize into the air we breathe. Their effects have been linked to headaches, nausea, dizziness, nerve damage and, in extreme cases, to liver and kidney disease. They are also suspected carcinogens. Low-VOC or VOC-free paints are now readily available in DIY stores.

For a green option, you can choose from a wide range of eco-paints and natural varnishes available from specialist and online distributors. These healthier alternatives to conventional paints include organic, milk (casein), water-based, natural or eco paint types. They use primarily natural solvents, such as citrus and other plant oils, and are free of preservatives and biocides. They tend to be more expensive than synthetic paints and often require more care and effort to mix and apply.

Lead-based paint has been banned in most western countries for many years but don't underestimate the danger from old and chipped lead paint in older properties. Never dry- or power-sand old paint. Lead poisoning is less likely if old paint is treated with a damp water-proof abrasive paper or with chemical stripper.

Choosing Floor Coverings

Expectant parents often decide to lay a new carpet in a baby's nursery as this is considered to be most hygienic. If you go down this route, make sure it is laid

at least a couple of months before the baby is going to use the room, because new synthetic carpets give off toxic fumes for quite some time after installation. By the same token, make sure you are not in the house while the carpet is being laid and get your partner or a friend to air the room well before you enter or spend any time in there.

A better option is to stick with natural fibre carpets, such as wool, but these can cost up to twice as much as their synthetic counterparts, and some may still have synthetic backings.

If you prefer to clean the existing carpet, then use topical treatments, such as anti-dust mite sprays (having first checked the packaging to make sure that they are safe to use when pregnant), and a vacuum cleaner with a fine-particle-trapping filter to control allergens. To deodorize carpets naturally, sprinkle with baking soda, leave for an hour, then vacuum.

Choosing Soft Furnishings

There are so many beautiful fabrics to choose from when fitting out a nursery – gorgeous quilts, sheets, blankets, cot bumpers, curtains. When trying to find the one that you love best, bear in mind that it makes best environmental sense to choose natural and untreated fabrics.

If you choose synthetic fabrics for curtains, the heat and light coming through the window will cause them to break down and give off gases into the room, which could be detrimental to you and to your baby once he

is sleeping there. Natural fabrics, such as cotton, linen and hemp, are the best choices for nursery curtains.

Blinds make suitable, non-allergenic alternatives to curtains. Whether it is made from steel, wood, bamboo or aluminium, ensure that the blind has not been chemically finished. If it has, allow it to aerate well away from you for a few days before installing.

Finally, it is worth bearing in mind that whereas these environmental considerations are important when decorating and furnishing your baby's first room, you should not worry about it to such an extent that it detracts from the pleasure of preparing the room for your new baby. Planning the nursery should be a joy for expectant parents, not a concern. Buying healthy and environmentally friendly decorating and furnishing options is obviously the best choice for optimum health for you and your baby, but even if you can implement just some of these recommendations, at least it's a step in the right direction.

Maternity Wear and Toiletries

No longer do pregnant women have to rely on wearing baggy, shapeless clothing to accommodate their bump. Now an impressive range of maternity clothes is available for both leisure- and business-wear, with many high-street fashion stores offering ranges for mums-to-be. Better yet, there are increasing numbers of outlets that stock or specialize in eco-friendly, organic maternity clothing, which is great news for green expectant mums.

Having said that, remember that the length of time when maternity clothes are a necessity is short. With the exception of buying just a few 'core' outfits, the best green option (and the best for your purse) is to borrow your maternity wardrobe from a friend and then pass it on to another pregnant friend when you've finished with it.

Bear in mind that your body temperature will increase with pregnancy, so you should favour clothes made from natural fibres, preferably organic and undyed or untreated cotton or wool, silk and cashmere. Unlike synthetics, natural fibres breathe and are less chafing.

When the weather turns cold, dress in layers that will draw the sweat away from your body – you can peel off or add layers as you please to regulate your temperature.

With the right clothing, you will feel more confident about your appearance and good about yourself.

Proper Support

When you are pregnant, your bra size can vary from two to four sizes larger. The increase in weight and size of the breasts during pregnancy will cause the skin to stretch and the breasts to drop, which is why it is important for pregnant women, however big or small your breasts, to be fitted for a new bra regularly (every couple of months). It is probably worth investing in some good maternity pants and tights, too, especially towards the end of your pregnancy. Not only are these extremely comfortable because they fit above your bump, but they also help to prevent varicose or spider veins and other leg problems.

DRY CLEANING

If you use a dry cleaner, ask if he uses PERC, benzene, sulphuric acid or toluene, chemicals that at high levels can cause headaches and faintness. Dry-cleaned clothes not exposed to these chemicals are safer.

When you pick up your clothes from the dry cleaners, make sure you ventilate them well, preferably outdoors, before wearing them.

---

greenfile

An ingenious clothing device that will extend the wear of your ordinary wardrobe well into your pregnancy is the pregnant tummy tube. It is a piece of stretchy fabric in a loop that supports your bump while also holding up your unbuttoned trousers and maintaining a stylish look. There are plenty to choose from but look out for those made of an environmentally sustainable material, such as bamboo.

Of course, your mother's solution to the same problem was an ever-lengthening elastic band threaded through the buttonhole and looped around the button of your trousers, coupled with a long top!

Cosmetics and Toiletries

Now is the time to take special care of your skin and to pamper yourself a little. Many women do seem to get a wonderful 'pregnancy glow' to their complexion, while others suddenly develop bad skin for the first time in their lives. Similarly, some unfortunate women suffer from stretch marks and others get away without so much as a blemish. How your skin reacts to pregnancy is something of a lottery. However, if you feed and treat your skin with natural products, rather than off-the-shelf cosmetics and toiletries that contain countless chemicals, you stand a better chance of continuing to have healthy vibrant skin throughout your pregnancy.

Skincare

There are so many lovely, natural and effective lotions and creams to keep your skin supple during your pregnancy that there is no need to choose conventional beauty products that contain parabens. These are a class of chemicals that are used as preservatives in cosmetics and toiletries. They are a cause of particular concern because you leave these products on your skin for a long time, so increasing exposure time. Some studies have linked the oestrogen-like effects of parabens to breast cancer and reproductive abnormalities, so it is well worth avoiding paraben-containing products in favour of organic or natural beauty products.

In fact, there is a plethora of small companies making a wonderful range of natural skincare lotions and creams especially for pregnant women. Always check out the list of ingredients used to assure yourself that their natural claims are authentic, and then treat yourself to a few items. If you would be happier rubbing only pure, unadulterated natural products into your skin, then the following oils, creams and unctions are recommended:

• vitamin E oil or lotion
• aloe vera gel
• wheatgerm or almond oil
• cocoa or shea butter
• calendula cream

greenfile

Antiperspirants containing aluminium chlorohydrate or/and aluminium zirconium chlorohydrate block skin pores and can cause inflammation. Choose a natural alternative containing ammonium alum or zinc ricinoleate, which are naturally occurring salts that will not cause any irritation and which 'fix' sweaty smells.

Haircare

Many women find that their hair tends to dry out during pregnancy, so after washing with a natural, non-toxic shampoo, apply a natural conditioner. The following recipe is a very easy one to make at home.

Peel one avocado and mash the flesh in a bowl. Add some coconut milk a little at a time while mashing with a fork. Keep blending until you reach the consistency of bottled conditioner. Apply by combing through the hair and leaving for 10–15 minutes before rinsing.

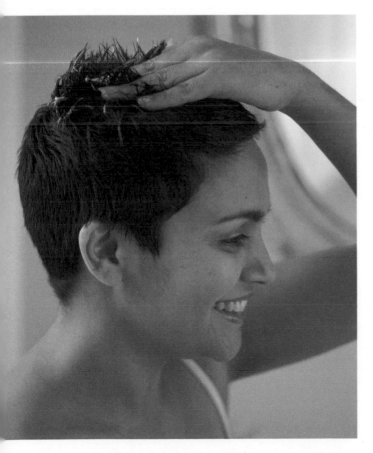

Dentalcare

Toothpastes containing ammonia, ethanol, formaldehyde, mineral oil or saccharin should be avoided. Instead, choose bicarbonate of soda, peppermint oil or natural herb toothpastes.

Tooth and gum problems are common, especially in the first half of pregnancy. Rather than using a conventional mouthwash after brushing, steep a chamomile tea bag in freshly boiled water for 15 minutes. When cooled, rinse around the mouth before spitting out. (See also page 131.)

Nailcare

If you are a big fan of a regular manicure or pedicure, you may not realize that conventional nail polish is one of the most toxic of all beauty products. Containing a mix of phthalates, formaldehyde and a host of other VOCs (volatile organic compounds), not to mention the acetone you need to remove old or chipping polish, your visit to the nail salon may be worth putting on hold.

However, in the last few years, a variety of non-toxic nail polishes has appeared on the market. Some are water-based and others use a natural mineral base but all allege to be toxin-free. Nonetheless, even with these new polishes, it is worth taking the precaution of having your nails done less frequently than usual and make sure the room is well ventilated.

CAMPAIGN FOR SAFE COSMETICS
For more information on body and face care, check out the Campaign for Safe Cosmetics in the UK and US. They have a 'Compact for Cosmetics', an agreement that over 600 companies who fit the criteria for safe products have signed. See Useful Contacts, page 156, for site details if you want to check whether your favourite cosmetics company has signed, making the products we put on our face and body healthier for us and our environment.

Prenatal Care

The first few weeks and months of pregnancy are so exciting yet, even as you are coming to terms with your news, you are faced with some early decisions that have to be made regarding what sort of pregnancy you would like, how you want to be cared for during this time, and what sort of birth you want for you and your baby.

There is a great deal of information available to you and a lot to digest in quite a short space of time. You may well have a clear idea of the overall approach you would like to take – and since you are reading this book, it is probably fair to assume that a natural attitude to pregnancy would best suit you – but you might be hazy on detail.

It is well worth reading about what's on offer both generally and in your locality, speaking to healthcare professionals and to other parents who have been through the experience personally before coming to any firm decisions.

This chapter looks at choosing the care provision that best suits your inclinations and needs (see page 86), the benefits of creating a birth plan (see page 89) and a review of the prenatal check-ups (see page 92) and testing (see page 96) that are on offer.

Finally, why not think about joining a childbirth education class (page 98) – there are classes to suit every taste, and some put more emphasis on a natural pregnancy and birth than others. However, classes can provide a great forum for you to explore all the issues about prenatal care and birth that interest you.

Choosing a Maternity Care Giver

Who you choose to look after you during your pregnancy will affect the experience you have and the care you receive. These antenatal professionals are responsible for your health and that of your baby throughout your pregnancy, so it is important to choose someone who is not only qualified and competent but whom you can trust and with whom you feel comfortable.

In the UK, the primary maternity care giver within the NHS system is your midwife. Midwives are specialists who are trained to provide maternity care where there are no medical complications. They will look after you throughout your pregnancy and you may not even see a doctor unless a problem arises. For other potential members of the antenatal care team, see opposite.

Hospital Birth

Some women feel reassured by having medical back-up close to hand, especially for a first baby. Others know that they will need medical intervention. In either case, the obvious choice is to book your birth in an obstetric or maternity unit of a hospital.

Under hospital antenatal care, you will probably be looked after by hospital midwives throughout your pregnancy and birth, or possibly by community midwives. This depends on the individual hospital and its provisions. In the case of any complications, an obstetrician is on hand to step in.

The approach of individual hospitals to continuity of care and giving you the birth experience that you want varies considerably. It is worth finding out how supportive your unit is likely to be and who is going to be looking after you. Options include:

Shared care where some of your antenatal appointments are with your GP and some at the hospital, with hospital midwives. You will be looked after by hospital midwives during labour and, after the birth, you will be visited by community midwives (sometimes from a different hospital from where you gave birth).

Team midwifery (aka caseload midwifery) means the hospital provides teams of community midwives who provide your antenatal care, care in hospital during your labour and birth, and visits at home after your baby has been born. This option often allows you to get to know the midwife who will be attending you at the birth.

Domino care is only offered by a small number of hospitals. Antenatal care is provided by community midwives, just as for a home birth. Your midwife will visit you at home during your labour and will accompany you to the hospital where you give birth. You then come home from hospital about six hours after the birth. Post-natal care is provided as for a home birth. This option is available only to women who are likely to have a straightforward birth because, if complications arise, your care would have to be handed over to hospital staff.

Midwifery Unit or Birth Centre

These units are run by midwives but they do not have all the medical facilities of a hospital unit. Since the majority of women can give birth without medical intervention, they can be a good halfway house between a hospital birth and a home birth.

> Some birth centres are next to a hospital maternity unit ('alongside') and others are completely separate from the hospital ('freestanding').

ANTENATAL CARE GIVERS

Within the NHS, there are two types of midwives, namely hospital and community midwives. Each provides maternity care but, as the name implies, hospital midwives work within a hospital environment, running antenatal clinics, helping you to give birth in hospital and looking after the antenatal and post-natal wards. They often work closely with doctors.

Community midwives, on the other hand, give maternity care in local clinics or visit women in their homes, although they are usually attached to a hospital or GP surgery. They attend home births, or may accompany you to hospital to give birth. They also visit you and your new baby at home for up to 28 days after the birth.

Alternatively, independent midwives work privately outside the NHS, providing continuity throughout your pregnancy and labour. Most attend births at home but they can accompany you to hospital if you need to transfer for care. Independent midwives charge for their services.

Your family doctor or GP may provide part of your antenatal care. This is called 'shared care' and it can be a good option if you enjoy a good relationship with your doctor or have ongoing medical problems.

Finally, an obstetrician is a hospital doctor who specializes in pregnancy and childbirth where there are problems. If you are one of the majority of women who are healthy with a normal pregnancy, you will not see an obstetrician.

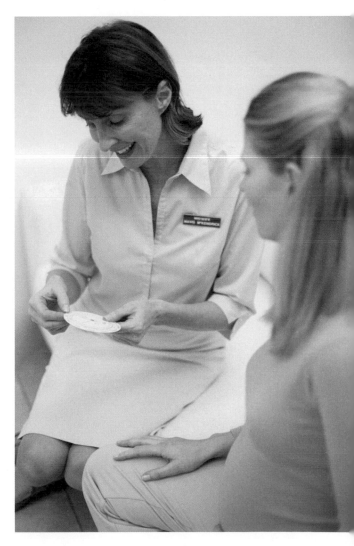

If you book to have your baby in an NHS birth centre, then you will have care with community midwives, which means you should benefit from continuity of care. As with a home birth, if problems arise, you may need to be transferred to the care of hospital midwives and doctors at the nearest hospital.

Birth centres tend to be more informal and relaxed than hospital units, and there are often birth pools, birth balls and birth cushions for use during labour. Although you cannot have an epidural for pain relief at a midwifery unit, the midwives are experienced and skilled at helping you to work with the pain of labour.

Home Birth

If you are a healthy woman and have enjoyed a normal pregnancy, then home birth is as safe as a hospital birth – and it is possible whether this is your first or your fifth baby.

If you book a home birth through the NHS, then you will be looked after by a small team of community midwives, assuring you of continuity of care. You will be assigned a named midwife from the team, whom you can get to know during your pregnancy, although you'll meet all the team members as well.

Your antenatal appointments will usually take place in your home or perhaps in a local clinic. When your labour starts, you contact your named midwife and she (or possibly another member of the team) will come to your home and care for you until the baby is born. Your midwife will then visit you regularly at home for between 10 and 28 days after your baby has been born.

If you are not sure whether you would prefer a home birth, you might find it helpful to talk to other people who have had home births in your area. They can tell you how easy or difficult it is to arrange a home birth there, and direct you towards any particularly helpful midwives. Talking to other people who have given birth at home can be a great confidence boost – it helps to know that there are lots of other women, just like you, who have done it. See Home Birth Support Groups in Useful Contacts on page 156, for further details.

greenfile

Evidence suggests that when antenatal care is midwife-led and birth takes place outside a consultant unit, intervention rates are lower. Moreover, studies show that babies born in birth centres find it easier to establish breast-feeding.

greenfile

Occasionally, women who want a home birth meet resistance from their GP or midwife. Carefully explain your reasoning and consider showing him/her a copy of the RCM and RCOG joint statement on home births available from their websites (see page 156).

If your doctor considers that you are not a good candidate for home birth, it is important to find out his/her specific reasons for this. You can then make an informed decision or seek advice elsewhere, for example from the Association for Improvements in the Maternity Services (AIMS). You can also get a second medical opinion or ask for a referral to an obstetrician where risk factors can be assessed.

Don't ignore the advice of your medical practitioners, but do make sure that your wishes are heard and fully understood before coming to a decision.

In April 2007, the Royal College of Midwives (RCM) and the Royal College of Obstetricians and Gynaecologists (RCOG) made a joint statement supporting home birth for women with uncomplicated pregnancies. In summary, it says that there is no reason why home birth should not be offered to women at low risk of complications and it may confer considerable benefits for them and their families. There is ample evidence showing that labouring at home increases a woman's likelihood of a birth that is both satisfying and safe, with implications for her health and that of her baby.

In 2006, the rate of home births in the US was 0.59 per cent of all births. This rate is comparable to that in other industrialized countries with two exceptions: England has experienced a rise in its home birth rate from 1.0 per cent in 1989 to 2.7 per cent in 2006, while the Netherlands has maintained astonishing rates of home birth of approximately 30 per cent.

Birth Plans

For those of you who are not familiar with the concept, a birth plan is a written outline of what you would ideally like to happen at your baby's birth. It's an opportunity to reiterate the things that are important to you. Your doctor and midwife will have it on hand at the birth to check what has been discussed and agreed with you during your pregnancy.

Whether or not you adhere strictly to your birth plan, its principal benefit is that it serves to focus your mind. In order to write a plan, you have to give serious consideration to the type of birth experience that you would most like and what this might involve. For example, do you want a hospital or home birth? What sort of pain relief would you prefer, if at all? Who do you want with you at the birth? Do you want any specialist equipment, such as a birthing pool or stool? And how would you like to welcome your newborn into the world?

To answer these questions, you must naturally rely on your intuition and personal preferences but you must also be well informed. And, to that end, writing a birth plan can prompt you to seek out reliable information and to ask pertinent questions of your midwife and other health professionals. You might also like to speak to friends who have recently had babies and get the benefit of their experiences.

Considerations

Clarity Bear in mind that the way you present the information in your birth plan can be just as important as the facts themselves. For example, you stand a better chance of ensuring that your wishes are met if you keep the contents concise, clear and easy to read. You should also be as precise as possible in stating what you want.
Flexibility Many women who have set their heart on a certain style of delivery, feel frustrated and disappointed when the birth does not go according to plan. Yet you should not feel that you have failed if you have not stuck exactly to your birth plan. The most

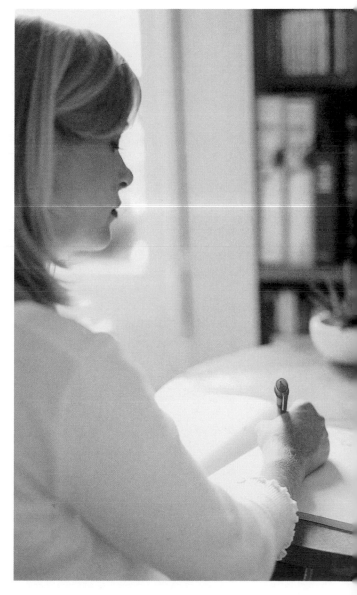

important advice to remember is to keep an open mind. Nobody can know how they are going to feel in labour until they get there. That's true even of women who have had babies before.

Experts agree that a birth plan is most effective if you remain flexible and recognize that it is a guideline rather than a bible. This approach avoids disappointment if events beyond your control mean your plans have to change and it also allows for the fact that you may feel very differently on the day. Staying open-minded gives you greater choice.

Healthcare conventions What is harder to accept is if the element of choice is removed. It may happen that you want to stick to your birth plan but this is made difficult, not for health reasons, but because of resistance from professionals involved in the birth or because of protocol. Occasionally, women report feeling that the hospital had let them down by not giving them the experience they wanted, despite assurances during their antenatal care.

Most hospitals now are far more accommodating of women who wish to have a natural or intimate birth experience, but not all. If your birth plan comprises anything that might be considered unconventional, for example:

- dimming of lights in the delivery room
- playing of relaxing music
- use of birthing pools, stools or other birthing aids
- resistance to electronic monitoring
- resistance to artificial rupture of membranes
- delivery while standing or kneeling

then you're best advised to discuss your wishes well in advance with the hospital.

Another way to improve the chances of compliance with your wishes is to include a statement in your birth plan saying: 'Do not perform the following without my express permission' and then to list the procedures over which you would like to be consulted.

A birth plan can bolster your resolve and give you the confidence to know your 'starting' position. You then have to be convinced of the case to take a different course of action.

Partner support It can also be useful to get your birth partner involved in dialogue and decision-making, since you may not be thinking clearly during labour. S/he can talk to staff and then talk to you. A birth partner should remain calm, think clearly and hopefully champion your case.

In most cases, it never comes to this and a birth plan is simply a useful tool to help you make certain decisions about the birth of your baby. Some antenatal notes even include a page for a birth plan. In general, it's perfectly acceptable to midwives, but not all women want to put their wishes down in writing. They prefer to wait and see what happens – and that's fine too.

Things to Think About: Labour

Birth partners Research shows that it's helpful to have someone, such as a partner, friend or relative, with you during your labour.

Carers Student midwives and medical students have to attend births as part of their training. Are you happy for students to be present?

Breaking your waters In some hospitals, the practice is to break the waters to speed up labour. Do you agree to having your waters broken artificially (see pages 143–4)?

Being induced Discuss with your midwife or doctor whether you want to be induced or not and what methods are available (see page 144).

Pain relief What's your position on self-help, such as moving around, changing positions, breathing techniques, relaxing in a bath or massage? Do you have a view on entonox (gas and air), TENS, pethidine or epidural? Is there a form of pain relief you definitely do not want to try (see page 147)?

Foetal monitoring Your midwife listens to the baby's heartbeat to detect any signs of distress. She may use a hand-held device or an electronic monitor, which can impede movement. In some hospitals, electronic monitoring is routine. What's the practice in your hospital? Do you have a preference?

Episiotomy This is a cut performed under local anaesthetic to enlarge the opening to the vagina and

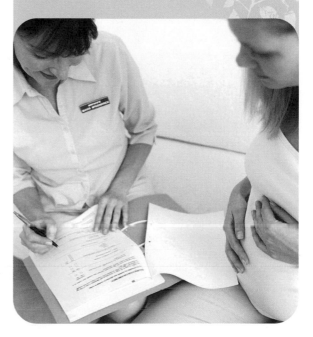

avoid natural tearing. If you are going to have a ventouse or forceps delivery, it will be performed automatically.

Things to Think About: The Birth

Assisted delivery Despite your best efforts, you may need help to deliver your baby safely. The doctor can explain the advantages and disadvantages of the methods available in your hospital so that you can choose.

Position for delivery Make it clear in which position you'd like to deliver your baby (see page 138).

Things to Think About: After The Birth

Cutting the umbilical cord Would you or your partner like to cut the cord? You can also ask to see the placenta after the birth.

The way your baby is delivered Do you want your baby placed on your stomach or lifted into your arms as soon as s/he is born? Research suggests that initial skin-to-skin contact can be beneficial to the bonding process.

Cleaning and bathing of your baby Would you like the midwife to clean and dry your baby and wrap him or her in a blanket?

Vitamin K Most British hospitals give newborn babies vitamin K in order to prevent a rare but serious blood

disorder, either by injection or by mouth. This is not compulsory.

Delivering the placenta Many hospitals offer a drug to separate the placenta from the womb after giving birth. If you do not want drugs, you must say so in advance so that a midwife who is experienced in 'non-active management' of the third stage can be involved.

Feeding your baby Do you want your baby put to the breast straight away?

The above information is food for thought only. You can include all or none of these points and you can, of course, add your own specific preferences and requirements to the plan.

Prenatal Check-ups

It is so exciting when you get a positive reading from a home pregnancy test kit and realize that you are expecting a baby. Once the initial euphoria has worn off, it is important to get your home-test results confirmed and to enter the health system that will monitor and help you throughout your pregnancy – and in most cases in the UK, this is the NHS.

Your First Appointment

In general, you should contact your local doctor's surgery to make an appointment with the midwife or doctor as soon as you discover that you are pregnant.

At this appointment, a pregnancy test will be done to confirm your own results. You will then be given information about:

- folic acid and vitamin D supplements (see pages 58–59)
- pregnancy nutrition and diet (see pages 42–63)
- food hygiene
- lifestyle factors that could affect you and/or your baby, such as smoking, drinking and recreational drug use (see pages 52 and 72)
- antenatal screening tests (see page 96)

At this first appointment, you should discuss with the midwife or doctor any family history (on either your or your partner's side) of inherited diseases, such as cystic fibrosis, if anyone in your family has previously had a baby with an abnormality, such as spina bifida, or if you are being treated for a chronic condition, such as diabetes or high blood pressure. If this is not your first pregnancy, you should also point out if you had any complications or infections in a previous pregnancy or delivery.

Thereafter, you will be given an initial 'booking appointment' followed by regular check-ups at which your health and your baby's development will be monitored. Antenatal appointments are reassuring, and also give you an opportunity to ask questions and to discuss any concerns or issues you may have.

Antenatal Schedule
Booking Appointment

Most women have their 'booking appointment', or 'booking-in', between the eighth and twelfth week of pregnancy. It can take a good couple of hours, as time is needed to assess you and your baby, to discuss your care and to give you information. At this appointment, you should receive information on:

- your baby's development during the pregnancy
- nutrition and diet
- exercise and pelvic-floor exercises
- antenatal screening tests
- your antenatal care
- antenatal classes
- maternity benefits
- planning your labour
- your options for where to have your baby

Your midwife or doctor should:

- give you your hand-held notes and plan of care
- identify any potential risks associated with your work
- measure your height and weight and calculate your body mass index

> **BOOKING IN**
> Go to see your doctor as soon as you know that you are pregnant, in order to get all the necessary checks and tests during your first trimester and to ensure that you are given an appointment for your first ultrasound scan. Ideally, booking-in should take place before 10 weeks.

- measure your blood pressure and test your urine for protein
- offer you screening tests, if applicable, and explain what's involved
- offer you an ultrasound scan at 8–14 weeks to estimate when your baby is due
- offer you an ultrasound scan at 18–20 weeks to check the physical development of your baby and screen for possible abnormalities
- take blood samples to check for blood group, haemoglobin levels (to check for anaemia), and immunity to rubella (if you have no immunity, you will be offered a post-natal vaccination). Diabetes, hepatitis, syphilis and your rhesus status will also be tested

You will be asked:
- the date of your last period
- your previous medical and family history, including previous births, miscarriages or abortions
- your partner's medical and family history (take him along too, if possible)

8–14 week ultrasound scan

Often known as a 12-week or dating scan, its main purpose is to work out how many weeks pregnant you are, and to estimate your due date. The scan can also check that your baby has a heartbeat and is developing normally and if you're expecting twins, triplets or more.

The scan takes about 5–10 minutes. The sonographer will put some gel on your tummy and will move a small hand-held device, called a transducer, over your skin to get views of your baby. Finally, you'll be given a report of the scan that will tell you exactly how many weeks pregnant you are.

Some hospitals offer a nuchal translucency scan to all women at 11–14 weeks. A nuchal translucency test is used to assess the risk of Down's syndrome and other chromosomal disorders. Using ultrasound to check for abnormal thickness in the fold at the back of the baby's neck (nuchal), this test (when combined with a blood test) is 80–90 per cent accurate in predicting Down's syndrome.

FOETAL HEARTBEAT

When you hear your baby's heartbeat for the first time, it is such an emotional moment. Usually from about 16 weeks onwards (sometimes earlier), your midwife may be able to listen to your baby's heartbeat. However, it is no longer recommended as part of routine antenatal appointments. This is because it can be uncomfortable if your midwife has to press into your bump to locate the heartbeat, and hearing the heartbeat doesn't tell you how healthy your baby is. However, if you want to hear your baby's heartbeat, your midwife can have a listen in for you, if you ask.

Some midwives use an old-fashioned Pinnard stethoscope, which looks like a small trumpet, to listen. She'll hold one end to your tummy and the other to her ear. However, most midwives now use a hand-held Sonicaid foetal heart monitor that amplifies your baby's heartbeat so you get to hear it, too. If you do get to hear the heartbeat, don't be surprised at the speed – your baby's heart rate is 120–160 beats per minute (BPM) compared to your 60–100.

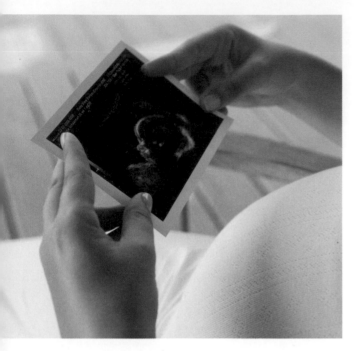

greenfile

Your blood pressure is lower in the middle of your pregnancy than at other times. It's perfectly normal but if you get up quickly, you may find yourself feeling slightly light-headed as a result.

16 week check-up

Your midwife or doctor will talk to you about the ultrasound scan and any screening tests that you have had, measure your blood pressure and test your urine for protein. If you are anaemic, an iron supplement may be considered. You may also discuss the 18–20 week ultrasound and any concerns or questions you may have about it.

REGULAR CHECKS

Your urine and blood pressure will be checked at every antenatal appointment.

Urine is analysed principally to check if protein or 'albumin' is present. If so, it may mean that you have an infection that needs treating. It can also be a sign of pre-eclampsia (high blood pressure).

A blood pressure reading of 140/90 or above in pregnancy indicates high blood pressure. A rise in blood pressure later in your pregnancy (combined with protein in your urine) could be a sign of pre-eclampsia, a complication that can cause premature labour and still birth if left untreated.

18–22 week ultrasound scan

You will be offered a detailed scan, known as the mid-pregnancy or anomaly scan, when you are between 18 and 22 weeks pregnant to check that your baby is developing normally, and to have a look at where the placenta is lying in your uterus. Measurements will be taken of your baby's head, spine, heart and other organs, hands, feet, arms and legs.

Most hospitals allow you to watch the scan, which takes about 15 minutes, as it is being performed and many allow you to buy a photograph of your unborn baby in the womb.

25 week check-up (first-time mothers only)

Your midwife or doctor will check the size of your uterus, measure your blood pressure and test your urine for protein.

28 week check-up

Using a tape measure, your midwife will measure the size of your uterus. Your blood pressure and a urine test will be taken. If you are rhesus negative, your first anti-D treatment will be offered (see right).

31 week check-up (first-time mothers only)

The size of your uterus will be measured, your blood pressure taken and a urine test for protein will be done. If you have had any screening tests since your last appointment, the results will be discussed.

34 week check-up

Your midwife or doctor should give you information about preparing for labour and birth, including how to recognize active labour, how to cope with pain in labour and your birth plan. S/he should also do the routine tests and measurements for the size of your uterus, blood pressure and urine. If you are rhesus negative, you will then be offered a second anti-D treatment.

36 week check-up

You will receive the routine checks for size of uterus, blood pressure and urine and the position of the baby will also be checked. You may discuss what happens after your baby is born, including feeding and caring for your newborn, vitamin K and screening tests for your baby, your own health after the baby is born, and post-natal depression and 'baby blues'.

38 week check-up

The size of your uterus will be measured, your blood pressure taken and your urine tested for protein. You might also discuss the options and choices available if your pregnancy lasts for more than 41 weeks.

40 week check-up (first-time mothers only)

This check-up is identical to the one you received at 38 weeks and is to reassure you and the medics that all is well.

41 week check-up

Naturally, no one wants to be at this check-up but if you run over your due dates, it is at this appointment that you will discuss the options and choices for induction of labour. You may also be offered a membrane sweep along with the routine tests and measurements for uterus size, blood pressure and urine.

ANTI-D TREATMENT

Blood tests will show if you are rhesus negative, but the medical team cannot know if your unborn child is rhesus positive or negative.

If your baby is rhesus positive and any of the baby's blood cells mix with yours, then your body may start to produce antibodies against the rhesus D positive factor (antigen). This is not usually dangerous in first pregnancies. However, these antibodies can cross the placenta and attack the blood cells of the unborn baby, causing haemolytic disease of the newborn (HDN). This is generally a mild condition but it can be more serious and cause anaemia or jaundice. Very rarely, it can cause stillbirth, severe disability or death after birth.

Anti-D treatment during your pregnancy is offered as a precaution and the implications and options available to you should be fully discussed so that you can make an informed decision about the treatment.

Antenatal Screening and Testing

All pregnant women are now routinely monitored throughout their pregnancy at antenatal visits, and tests that were once performed only if problems were suspected are now used more commonly. Some of the screening tests are more invasive than others.

A natural practitioner would recommend the use of basic tests that are performed at an antenatal visit, for example, urine testing, checking blood pressure, measuring the growth of the uterus abdominally using a tape measure and listening to the baby's heartbeat with a Pinnard stethoscope (see page 93).

However, those who favour a natural approach to prenatal care have reservations about the use of invasive – and they would say sometimes unreliable – procedures that have become routine in some places.

These antenatal screening tests to detect foetal abnormalities have their place and can prove extremely useful, depending on the circumstances. Not only can it be an immense relief to find out your baby is growing well, for example, but screening can also provide life-saving information when a problem is suspected.

However, it is also important that every woman knows that antenatal testing is not obligatory and that she educates herself about the advantages and disadvantages of each test so that both she and her partner can make up their own minds about which tests they want done and which to refuse, if they deem it unnecessary.

Before making a decision about whether or not to undergo a test, it is also worth considering what you might do with the information if the test results were positive. You must weigh the risks and benefits of having these tests, especially if you plan to keep the baby no matter what the problem is. Support and counselling are available for all parents in these emotionally difficult situations (see Useful Contacts, page 156).

OLDER MOTHERS

In developed countries there is a noticeable upsurge in the age of mothers giving birth for the first time, and in the UK alone there are now more first-time mothers giving birth in the 30–34 age group than in the 25–29 age group. There is also a 50 per cent increase from ten years ago in the number of women aged 40–44 who are having a baby.

Unfortunately, the odds of having a baby with a genetic defect do increase as you get older. Figures from the Office of National Statistics, for 2005, show that the risk of having a baby with a genetic abnormality, such as Down's syndrome, rises from 2 per 1,000 births at ages 35–39 years, to 4 per 1,000 at age 40–44 years up to 14 per 1,000 at age 45 years or over.

If you're almost, or over, 40, you should strongly consider genetic testing, such as chorionic villus sampling, amniocentesis (see right) or the quadruple tests, because the risk of genetic problems increases significantly. Your care giver can give you full details of what these tests involve and the risks they may incur.

However, bear in mind, also, that many women who have delayed pregnancy until they're over 35 are surprised to find that, given generally good health, they're not much more likely than younger women to have serious complications, and the vast majority of women end up having healthy babies.

Chorionic Villus Sampling (CVS)

This procedure is used to detect chromosomal and genetic disorders, such as Down's syndrome and sickle-cell anaemia. At 8–12 weeks, a tube is inserted through the abdomen or cervix and tissue is taken from the uterus and the tissue surrounding the embryo.

Advantages Accurate results within 48 hours.

Disadvantages Possible damage to the embryo, cervix and uterus with an approximate risk of miscarriage of 1 in 100.

Amniocentesis

Under local anaesthetic, a long, sterile needle is inserted through your abdominal and uterine walls into the amniotic fluid and a sample is taken. This test is conducted at 16–18 weeks to provide information about certain birth defects, such as Down's syndrome and cystic fibrosis. Results take about 2–3 weeks.

Advantages Extreme accuracy (c. 90 per cent) and for gender-related disorders, it reveals the baby's sex.

Disadvantages Amniocentesis cannot screen for all defects and it can cause miscarriage (less than 1 per cent). It can also cause discomfort and side effects, such as bleeding and infection.

Alpha-Fetoprotein Test (AFP)

This blood test checks blood protein levels and can detect neurological problems, such as spina bifida or hydrocephalus.

Advantages Non-invasive with no side effects.

Disadvantages Although not harmful, this test has a high rate of false positives and is only 50 per cent accurate. You are then frequently referred for further screening – probably an amniocentesis – with a higher risk factor.

greenfile

The optimum time to perform an AFP test is between 15 and 18 weeks when the test is thought to be most accurate.

ULTRASOUND SCANNING

The vast majority of British and American women have at least one scan during pregnancy and probably two, but it is not compulsory. If you'd rather not have a scan, then you should discuss this with your midwife and the final decision rests with you. However, it is worth bearing in mind that ultrasound scans give reliable and useful information about your pregnancy and, for many women, it is reassuring to see your baby moving on screen.

There has been a growth in the number of private clinics that are offering obstetric scans and both 3D and 4D ultrasound scan technology is now widely available.

The 3D ultrasound produces a life-like picture of your baby built up from images of the three 'planes' of vision as stored in the computer after the ultrasound. A 4D ultrasound is a moving or 'video-style' image of your baby in the womb.

Apart from the financial considerations (it is not cheap), there is no restraint on how many private scans an expectant mother can undergo. However, although there is no medical evidence that ultrasound scanning can harm an unborn child, some believe that more long-term research is needed.

As a result of this lack of research, some experts suggest that the ultrasound scanning is more appropriately reserved for essential, diagnostic use only, for example to investigate a suspected placenta previa (when the placenta is lying unusually low in the uterus), to assess a baby with a significant size/dates discrepancy, to determine foetal position if palpation cannot establish this, and if it is suspected that the baby might have died in the womb.

Natural Birth Education Classes

Antenatal classes, or birth education classes as they are also known, are a very good way to prepare yourself for your baby's birth and to meet other pregnant women who are due around the same time as you and in your local area.

Depending on the type of class you choose, you may well be able to find out more about arrangements for labour and birth in your particular locality. Local NHS classes are sometimes run by the midwives who will be looking after you during labour, which is another added bonus.

First-time mothers, in particular, enjoy the opportunity of talking to other women as well as professionals about their worries and concerns, and discussing their plans with others in the same situation can be a real help. Depending on the topic being discussed that week, partners are also welcome at some classes and this can be illuminating for both of you, because you may find you can talk more openly in a group discussion.

Naturally, the information and support you gain from these classes can really help you to make informed decisions about the sort of labour and birth you might like to have. However, another added and not inconsiderable benefit is that antenatal classes are a wonderful way to make friends with local women in similar situations and at the same stage in life that you have reached – and you'd be surprised how often these friendships can help you immensely through the first few months of living with a new baby. Some can last a lifetime.

Choosing an Antenatal Class

You should have some intuitive idea of what you would like to gain from an antenatal class so that you can choose the sort of class that best suits your needs, such as a class that embraces natural birth options and pain relief, or one that concentrates more on a conventional approach.

THE NCT

The National Childbirth Trust, or NCT as it is more commonly known, runs a range of antenatal classes ranging from standard courses to refresher classes for those women who have already had a baby but want to build on their past experience.

The groups tend to be smaller and go into considerable depth, often allowing time for discussion and for practising practical skills. Prices vary according to length of course and subject matter.

For further details, check out their website (see Useful Contacts, page 156).

Start looking for a class quite early in your pregnancy since places get booked up well in advance. You can, of course, choose more than one class, if you want a broader take on your options.

Talk to your midwife, health visitor or doctor about what is available. As well as NHS antenatal courses (which are free), there are private courses available, or contact the National Childbirth Trust (see above).

Many antenatal classes also cover breast-feeding and early baby care.

What to Expect

Classes are usually held once a week and last for about two hours, either during the day or in the evening. The atmosphere is generally relaxed and informal. Some classes are open to women only. Other courses welcome all parents and parents-to-be, including young parents, women without a partner, same-sex couples and surrogacy couples. Women who are not attending with a partner are usually welcome to bring someone else along to classes, for example a friend or family member.

Most women start attending about 8–10 weeks before their baby is due. Bear in mind that if you're expecting twins (or more), then you might like to start the classes earlier since you'll probably deliver before your due date.

The range of topics usually covered in antenatal education includes:

- health in pregnancy
- suitable exercises during labour
- what happens during labour and birth
- coping with labour and different types of pain relief
- self-help techniques for labour and birth
- relaxation techniques
- how to give birth without intervention, if that's what you want
- information on different kinds of birth and intervention
- emotional changes in pregnancy, and the early post-natal period
- your health after the birth
- caring for your new baby, including feeding

Not all classes are able to cover all of the above topics – some choose to concentrate on certain aspects, so it's worth checking course content before booking.

Remedies & Therapies

There are numerous complementary therapies and natural treatments available that can help to relieve many of the common ailments of pregnancy, helping you to enjoy the optimum mental and physical health possible.

Complementary therapies can help you prepare for the birth, provide pain relief in labour, ease nursing difficulties and help you through the early days of parenthood. Yet it brings peace of mind to know that modern obstetric and paediatric doctors are available should the need arise. An integrated approach, combining conventional antenatal care provision with complementary therapies, can often bring the best and most pleasing results.

In this chapter, we seek to give you a basic overview of some of the complementary practices that are most appropriate during pregnancy so that you can confidently choose the therapy that is right for you.

The therapies range from manipulative treatments that involve a hands-on approach, such as reflexology or osteopathy, through energy therapies, such as reiki and use of flower essences, to medicinal therapies that involve taking drops, tinctures or teas, such as homeopathy and herbalism.

Each therapy has its own governing body and it is essential that you check the credentials of any practitioner – make sure that they have the right qualifications and insurance, and follow the code of ethics. For further details on a particular therapy or for a list of local practitioners, contact the relevant individual association (see Useful Contacts, page 156).

Chiropractic

Chiropractic treatment involves manipulating the body's joints, with emphasis on the spine, in order to relieve irritation on the nerves that run through the centre of the spinal column. Considered an alternative medicine since its development at the end of the nineteenth century, its benefits are now more widely recognized by medical practitioners. Chiropractors believe that if a vertebra is displaced, it may press against nerves and so cause an imbalance, resulting in discomfort, pain or even disease.

greenfile

Chiropractors who routinely treat pregnant women usually have a chiropractic table with a break away pelvic/abdominal section. When your bump becomes too big for you to lie face down comfortably, this allows your belly and consequently the baby to remain unrestricted during the adjustment. After the fourth to fifth month, you should never lie on your stomach for an adjustment without this type of table, or without the use of a pregnancy cushion or pillow.

BENEFITS OF CHIROPRACTIC

Pregnancy: Chiropractors can help relieve spinal or back problems caused by physical and chemical changes in a woman's body when she is pregnant. Treatment can also relieve symptoms of nausea, sciatica, and lower back and pelvic pain, especially in late pregnancy. A chiropractor may also offer advice on how to adapt your lifestyle in order to make daily routines easier.

Post-natal mothers: Treatment is recommended for back problems associated with a difficult birth, reduced sleep and lifting the new baby. Childbirth can also cause your upper back musculature to become tight, interfering with proper nerve flow to the breasts. By chiropractic adjustment of the spine following delivery, milk can flow properly, decreasing breast-feeding problems.

Chiropractic treatment is drug-free and uses gentle pressure and manipulation of the spine to relieve painful conditions. Realigning the spine during pregnancy releases uterine nerves so that they can function properly. Treatment is carried out by means of precise adjustments, in a similar way to osteopathy (see opposite). There are many similarities between the two therapies but a slight difference lies in the emphasis placed on soft tissue and spinal manipulation techniques. Chiropractors are also trained to take and read X-rays.

What to Expect at a Consultation

After taking details of your medical history, a chiropractor will ask you to adopt various positions in order to evaluate your spinal function. He will use gentle manipulation to correct any misalignment and may use a gentle thrust to free a joint.

Chiropractors are able to give tips on proper back exercises and nutrition to help you have a comfortable and healthy pregnancy. Depending on your condition, you can expect to attend for up to six sessions, or for routine visits each month. A chiropractor who is versed in the needs of pregnant women will also provide you with exercises and stretches that are safe to use during pregnancy and complement any adjustments made to your spine.

Osteopathy

Osteopathy uses manipulative techniques and massage to restore and maintain the musculo-skeletal system (the bones, joints, muscles, ligaments and connective tissue), easing muscle tension and restoring joint mobility and balance. Since your changing shape and increasing weight affect this balance, osteopathy may be of real benefit in relieving the aches and pains of pregnancy.

There are several specializations within osteopathy, including cranial osteopathy, which uses very small movements and manipulation of the head. These work with the anatomy and physiology of the patient to effect changes and to allow health to be restored.

What to Expect at a Consultation

After taking a full medical history and reviewing your lifestyle and your emotional health, an osteopath will check your posture, mobility and weight distribution. He will then form a diagnosis and treatment plan that may include manipulation and massage.

An osteopath can monitor your changing body throughout your pregnancy, making adjustments as necessary, with a final appointment six weeks after the birth of your baby.

Treatment may consist of massage, manipulation, stretching and, occasionally, what is known as the 'high velocity thrust' – a vigorous technique used to free up a joint, although this is not commonly used during pregnancy. Treatment is not usually painful although it can feel a little uncomfortable.

> **BENEFITS OF OSTEOPATHY**
>
> **Pregnancy:** With its emphasis on maintaining the musculo-skeletal system, osteopathy is most often used to relieve backache during pregnancy but it is also helpful for correcting 'pregnancy posture', and treating morning sickness, piles, swollen legs and hands and for moving the baby into a more comfortable position. In the latter stages of pregnancy, osteopathy can help sciatica, pubic pain, ligament pain, restricted mobility, swollen ankles (oedema) and carpal tunnel syndrome.
>
> **Post-natal mothers:** Osteopathy is used to help both mother and baby recover after the shock of the birth, and treatment is sometimes available in the hospital in the days following delivery. In the few months after giving birth, problems such as stress-incontinence or shoulder pain from breast-feeding can also benefit from osteopathic treatment.

According to a recent survey, more than 80 per cent of mums-to-be experience back pain at some time during their pregnancy.

WARNING Although osteopathy is safe throughout pregnancy, many osteopaths avoid giving treatment at the transition from the first to the second trimester (about 12 weeks) because this is a vulnerable time.

Reflexology

Loosely based on ancient eastern foot massage therapies, western reflexology involves the gentle manipulation of the feet (or occasionally hands) to stimulate the body's own healing process.

The underlying principle is similar to that of acupuncture (see page 108) in that each pressure point on the sole or sides of the foot correlates to a particular function or part of the body. However, the meridians or zones of the body are described differently in reflexology from the way they are described in acupuncture. In reflexology, every organ and system of the body has a corresponding 'reflex point'.

Reflexologists believe that by applying pressure to specific points on the foot, this stimulates the corresponding part of the body to get rid of toxins, allowing the body to heal itself.

Reflexology is suitable for a wide range of pregnancy conditions but is particularly appropriate for any circulation or stress-related problems and for pain management.

What to Expect at a Consultation

Although reflexology is not a diagnostic tool, it does look at the underlying causes for symptoms, so your initial treatment will probably address you as a whole rather than purely your specific ailment.

Reflexology is a non-invasive therapy and you will merely be asked to take off your shoes and socks. The treatment should be relaxing as the therapist exerts a firm pressure with the thumb on each reflex point, working from toe towards ankle. However, you may experience some pricking pain occasionally or a bruised sensation as an area that correlates to an affected organ or region is worked on.

Some people experience a slight reaction to treatment the following day – perhaps mild flu-like symptoms or a slight skin rash. This is a sign that the body is beginning to detoxify and heal itself and they should pass fairly quickly. Another common side effect is more frequent urination after a treatment – something you know all about when you're pregnant anyway. Weekly sessions are recommended, usually for about six weeks, depending on the condition. Each session lasts about an hour.

greenfile

Reflexology can work extremely well alongside orthodox treatment for common pregnancy ailments.

BENEFITS OF REFLEXOLOGY

Pregnancy: Reflexology has a good track record for treating conditions such as stress, backache, morning sickness, headache, constipation, cystitis and raised blood pressure.

Labour: Great for pain control when giving birth and to reduce the length of labour.

Post-natal mothers: Again, good for control of chronic pain and dealing with the discomforts and minor conditions associated with the period just after giving birth.

WARNING Reflexology is not suitable if you have a history of miscarriage or if there's a risk of foetal loss, pre-eclampsia or placental disturbance. Care should be taken in the first trimester of pregnancy and you must tell your practitioner that you are pregnant. You should consult a qualified practitioner before attempting any self-help techniques.

Aromatherapy

Aromatherapy uses essential plant oils to improve physical, mental and emotional health and to prevent disease. The oils can be administered by massage, inhalation, compressions and/or baths.

Essential oils can be very potent, and not all are safe to use during your pregnancy (see below). It is therefore important to find a qualified aromatherapy practitioner who can recommend particular oils to treat your condition, and give indications of the doses to be used. You can choose to benefit from aromatherapy by inhaling the oils or via an aromatherapy massage (see page 38).

What to Expect at a Consultation

After a discussion about your medical and lifestyle history, an aromatherapy practitioner will select oils for their specific effects and may blend as many as five oils together for optimum results. These oils are then diluted in a carrier oil, such as sweet almond oil, before being applied to your skin, usually in the form of a therapeutic massage.

Note that the following oils should be avoided during pregnancy: aniseed, arnica, basil, clary sage, cypress, fennel, jasmine, juniper, marjoram and rosemary.

BENEFITS OF AROMATHERAPY

Pregnancy: Oils can be used to ease symptoms such as lower back pain and to give temporary relief from sciatica. They are also beneficial for stress relief and relaxation. When working in conjunction with GPs and midwives, aromatherapy can be used to help oedema, or swelling.

Labour: Some oils can assist with the labour and have an effect on the uterus and uterine muscles. For instance, jasmine helps the uterine muscles and also gives confidence. If you don't want to be massaged, you can always burn oils in the delivery room to good effect. If a burner is not permitted, oils will vaporize well in hot water in a small room.

Post-natal mothers: If you have stitches, a few drops of lavender oil in the bath are very beneficial due to its natural healing and antiseptic qualities. Geranium also helps with hormone balance. These oils must be used in a very low dilution while you are breast-feeding.

Many pregnant women have successfully used aromatherapy on themselves during their pregnancy to alleviate common ailments but caution must be exercised. You should always use the best quality organic oils you can buy and follow instructions carefully. Consult your midwife or doctor before using essential oils.

greenfile

Mothers report that regular aromatherapy massage during pregnancy results in babies who are calm and good sleepers.

WARNING Some essential oils should not be used for the first 14–16 weeks of pregnancy and some remain contra-indicated throughout the full term (see above). A qualified aromatherapy practitioner can give details of dilutions for massage but these are generally very low during pregnancy (about 5 drops of essential oil to 4 tablespoons of carrier oil) and for infants. Expert advice should always be sought and followed.

Acupuncture

One of the best known and respected of complementary therapies, acupuncture is in fact part of the comprehensive system of Traditional Chinese Medicine (TCM) that dates back thousands of years. However, in the West, acupuncture is often used in isolation and many conventional health professionals have learnt the techniques.

The philosophy behind TCM and acupuncture is completely different from western medical thinking. According to Chinese belief, the key to health lies in the balance of two opposing forces (yin and yang, the passive and active force). Achieving balance and harmony is the fundamental objective of this complex and sophisticated system of medicine. It emphasizes the close interaction of mind and body.

Healthy balance relies on the smooth flow of vital energy known as qi (pronounced 'chee') through channels or meridians in the body. Imbalance or ill-health occurs when there are blockages or weaknesses in the flow of this energy, or if outside influences, such as excessive heat, cold or damp, get into the body.

Acupuncture involves using very fine needles, inserted at strategic points (acupoints) on the body to stimulate the flow of vital energy and to correct imbalances. There are other non-invasive alternatives (see right).

What to Expect at a Consultation

Treatment is preceded by very careful questioning and observation. The practitioner will look at how you move, your complexion, body shape, and so on. He will listen carefully not only to the answers to his questions but to how you answer – your tone and how you respond. The practitioner will closely inspect your tongue and will also feel the six pulses on your wrists (three on each according to TCM) and will take down details of your medical history, lifestyle, sleep patterns, eating habits, likes and dislikes.

From this, he will decide on a course of treatment, often using a combination of acupuncture, herbs and

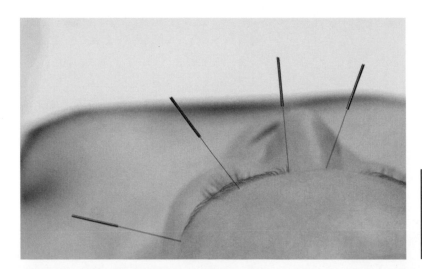

WARNING Make sure you inform your practitioner that you are pregnant before treatment commences as certain acupoints should not be stimulated during pregnancy.

occasionally moxibustion (where herbs are burnt over an acupoint without touching the skin). You generally require between six to ten treatments before you see improvement in your condition.

Although it is natural to worry about whether having needles stuck in you may hurt, actually all you should feel is a pinprick as the needles are inserted and perhaps a slight sensation of tingling or numbness. Initially, the needles are left in for 6–10 minutes, building to 20 or 25 minutes in later sessions. Don't be surprised if you feel somewhat sleepy after a session – this is entirely normal.

greenfile

The name moxibustion is derived from the Chinese word for mugwort, moxa, which is the herb that is dried and burned in the treatment.

BENEFITS OF ACUPUNCTURE OR ACUPRESSURE

Pregnancy: Either treatment can help relieve common pregnancy problems, such as morning sickness, nausea, constipation, haemorrhoids, varicose veins, heartburn and backache, and are also effective against many conditions that you may have had prior to pregnancy for which you can no longer take medication, such as stress-related problems or migraine.

Labour: Often used when breech presentations need turning and for those who have gone over term and don't want to be induced. Treatment starts around week 41 and during the days between then and going into hospital for an induction. Sometimes an acupuncturist will go into hospital once the waters have broken to try to get the labour going.

However, acupuncture and/or acupressure are mainly used during labour for pain relief and can have a significant effect – ideal if you want a totally natural birth. Acupuncture can also be used to help the placenta deliver naturally without the need for an injection.

Post-natal mothers: Acupuncture is very successful in the treatment of haemorrhoids. It is also useful to help you get your strength back and to treat physical problems, such as mastitis, as well as emotional problems, such as 'baby blues' or even post-natal depression.

ACUPRESSURE

If you are concerned by the idea of having needles inserted into you, acupressure is an effective alternative whereby the therapist applies gentle pressure to the acupoints in place of needles.

In recent years, laser or ultrasound acupuncture has also become more popular, since with these new techniques, nothing actually breaks the skin.

Reiki

Reiki is a form of healing therapy that was devised in Japan in the early twentieth century by Dr Mikao Usui, after years of research and meditation. It is primarily used for stress reduction and relaxation and to promote healing.

Reiki practitioners are trained to channel reiki healing energy through their hands to wherever it is needed in the patient's body. They achieve this by laying their hands on or over specific areas of your body.

The treatment is able to address physical, mental, emotional and spiritual problems and to stimulate your body's own healing powers to restore balance. Reiki practitioners believe that the body absorbs the help that it needs and that the healing energy travels directly to the source of the problems, giving relief from symptoms, deep relaxation, and mental and emotional harmony.

What to Expect at a Consultation

A treatment usually lasts about an hour. The practitioner will ask you to lie with your eyes closed on a raised couch (you remain fully clothed) or occasionally to sit on an upright chair. The practitioner then holds her hands on or just above your body, moving them to various positions where her hands may remain for sometime before moving on.

BENEFITS OF REIKI

Pregnancy: Reiki is helpful in easing back pain, sciatica and headaches, and for dealing with emotional conditions, such as anxiety and stress. It is also said to be good for preparing the body and mind for the birth.

Post-natal mothers: Reiki is believed to help relieve emotional 'blockages' and to help you to deal with any negative thoughts.

greenfile

Reiki has grown in popularity at a remarkable rate in recent years and there are many newly qualified practitioners with limited experience. Make sure you consult a reiki master who is well practised and who knows that you are pregnant (see Useful Contacts, page 156).

WARNING Currently, there is no formal accreditation of reiki training based on approved national standards in the UK. Until national standards for reiki are developed and a register of professional practitioners is in place, you should exercise caution when choosing a practitioner. Wherever possible, go on personal recommendation.

Hypnotherapy

Hypnosis works with your subconscious mind to help overcome unwanted habits of physical responses. Your conscious mind can focus on only one or two things at once, whereas your subconscious is much bigger and is constantly processing information and storing it.

Hypnotherapy is growing in popularity for pregnant women because it is completely non-invasive, it has no side effects and can be used safely when other options are limited.

If you have an emotional concern, such as a fear of childbirth or a needle phobia, you could benefit from hypnotherapy. In addition, hypnotherapy can help with physical problems, such as heartburn, water retention and nicotine- or alcohol-dependency. For help during labour, hypnobirthing is now a recognized option (see page 148).

Self-hypnosis techniques can be taught to you by a hypnotherapist, which can be useful for deep relaxation and relieving stress.

What to Expect at a Consultation

The practitioner will talk to you about your health and any problems you may be encountering. You will then be put into a hypnotic state, where you will feel deeply relaxed while your practitioner talks to you in a slow, soothing voice. It's likely that you will be fully aware of everything going on around you but you will feel at ease. Contrary to popular belief, a hypnotherapist cannot make you do anything you don't want to do and you can stop the session at any time.

greenfile
Under hypnosis, you can visualize your baby rather like a 3D scan but in your own mind.

WARNING Always consult a fully qualified, registered hypnotherapist (see Useful Contacts, page 156).

BENEFITS OF HYPNOTHERAPY
Pregnancy: Excellent results with discomfort, high blood pressure, heartburn, water retention, stress and anxiety, fear of the birth, needle phobias and addictions, such as helping you to give up smoking or alcohol.
Labour: Useful for turning breech babies, for natural induction and for preparing for a Caesarean section.
Post-natal mothers: Helpful for rapid healing after birth, post-natal depression and bonding with your baby.

Studies in the USA and Australia show that hypnosis can help with relaxation, post-natal depression and managing discomfort. Some hospitals in Australia have begun working with hypnotherapists in antenatal support.

Research published in the British Medical Journal showed that nicotine in patches can still cross the placenta – however, hypnosis is a completely safe way of trying to quit smoking.

Medical Herbalism

During your pregnancy, you may be drawn to herbalism as a non-toxic alternative to conventional medicines. In fact, herbs have been used for thousands of years to ease pregnancy symptoms and the pain of labour.

Modern scientific interest in herbalism stems from a growing awareness that man-made drugs may have unpleasant, and sometimes serious, side effects. Many doctors accept the validity of herbalism and may refer patients on the NHS in the UK, particularly for chronic conditions. Meanwhile, extensive research is being carried out into the plant-based folk medicines of the native peoples of South America, Africa, China, Siberia and elsewhere.

Today, scientists find, extract and then synthesize in the laboratory a single active constituent from a plant – the part that has therapeutic value. That ingredient is then manufactured on a large scale for use in pharmaceutical drugs. Herbal drugs, however, are extracts from sections of the whole plant, such as leaves, roots, berries, and contain hundreds, perhaps thousands, of plant constituents.

Herbalists believe that the active constituents are balanced within the plant and are made more (or less) powerful by the numerous other substances present. For example, synthetic diuretics seriously reduce the potassium levels in the body, and this is restored using potassium supplements. The herbalist uses dandelion leaves, which are potent diuretics but also contain potassium to replace naturally that which is lost.

Each culture has its herbal tradition, but Chinese herbal medicine is now proving to be very popular in the West, particularly for the treatment of skin problems. Traditional Chinese medicine works with about 10,000 different herbs, often used in conjunction with acupuncture (see page 108). Western herbalists follow the same principles, using different, indigenous plants.

While Chinese herbs are especially popular for treatment of skin problems, practitioners can treat

BENEFITS OF MEDICAL HERBALISM

Pregnancy: Many of the usual complaints that crop up during pregnancy, such as morning sickness, constipation, headaches, tiredness, skin problems and haemorrhoids, will respond to herbal treatment, when prescribed by a professional.

Labour: Increasingly women are using herbs in the form of herb teas, tinctures or essential oils to facilitate a smooth labour. If you want to use herbs during labour to influence contractions (hypertonic or stalled for example), you should consult a practitioner. A professional, who can reliably liaise with other health professionals if necessary, will then be on hand throughout your care.

Post-natal mothers: You can use herbs after the birth of your baby for physical and emotional support. There are herbs to aid recovery from the impact of giving birth, to help wound healing, to strengthen the system when the demands of breast-feeding hit you, and to soothe frazzled nerves when it all feels too much!

Useful herbs to enhance milk flow in breast-feeding mothers are raspberry, fennel and nettle. Herbs for lifting the spirits include lemon balm, lavender and St John's wort. However, significant, prolonged post-natal depression needs to be treated by a qualified practitioner.

WARNING Although some plant-based treatments for minor ailments – particularly herb teas or infusions – are widely available and are generally regarded as harmless, other plant derivatives are potentially dangerous and should be administered only under the guidance of a professional medical herbalist. Certain plants and herbs should be avoided during pregnancy and anyone with liver disease, such as hepatitis, or high blood pressure should consult a doctor before taking Chinese herbs.

all physical conditions that don't require surgery or manipulation, and psychological problems as well. Many conditions are treated with a combination of herbs and acupuncture: the acupuncture relieves immediate symptoms, while the longer-term herbal treatment will restore the balance of the body.

What to Expect at a Consultation

In Chinese medicine, the diagnosis will be made from looking at your tongue, taking the pulses in the wrists and observing your general appearance. Western medical herbalists are trained in the same diagnostic skills as orthodox doctors but take a more holistic approach to illness. The underlying cause of the problem is sought and, once identified, it is this that is treated rather than the symptoms alone.

Herbal treatments may be prescribed in the form of a tincture (an alcohol-based liquid), a cream or compress, or a dried herb powder from which to make up a tea. This should be taken several times a day as prescribed. Treatment may include advice about diet and lifestyle as well as the herbal medicine.

HERBAL SELF-HELP

There are certain gentle tea infusions that may be taken in moderation throughout pregnancy. For example, you can sip ginger tea made from fresh root ginger steeped in hot water to quell the nausea of morning sickness. Similarly, chamomile tea for relaxation is safe throughout. However, as a general rule of thumb, take herbal or plant remedies only under professional supervision.

On the other hand, herbal compresses and poultices are completely safe, yet very beneficial, because they are applied topically. For example, a cold witch hazel or nettle tea compress applied directly to haemorrhoids brings immediate relief.

Some women swear that taking raspberry leaf (*Rubus idaeus*) as a herbal tea can bring on labour and make it easier, and even that it can help to restore the uterus to its non-pregnant state after the birth.

Homeopathy

As a non-toxic alternative to conventional pharmaceutical drugs, it is no surprise that homeopathy is such a popular choice of treatment for pregnant women. Homeopathy was founded by a German doctor, Samuel Hahnemann, in 1796. It is based on the belief that 'like may cure like' – a theory similar to that underlying vaccination or immunization, where the body's natural resistance is stimulated by a remedy that mimics the symptoms.

The basis of homeopathic treatment is to stimulate the body's own healing processes to cure the particular ailment or overpower the bacteria, rather than treating the symptoms themselves.

Homeopaths emphasize that they treat people rather than diseases and that a human being is more than the sum of his physical parts. Homeopathic medicine is said to be suitable for both acute and chronic conditions.

A minute amount of the active ingredient is used in a specially prepared form, which means homeopathic remedies cannot cause side effects and you cannot become addicted to them. Many of the remedies are produced from herbs or plants, although conventional drugs can also be prescribed homeopathically, that is in very small amounts. Homeopaths believe the more dilute the concentration, the more powerful and effective it is.

What to Expect at a Consultation

Your homeopath will start by taking a detailed case study, including your past medical history and finding out about your general energy levels. An initial consultation may last an hour or more. Your homeopath will then prescribe a homeopathic remedy, usually in tablet or powder form for adults, or as a liquid remedy for infants. Further appointments last about half an hour.

During treatment, you may experience a period of exceptional well-being and optimism. Alternatively, you may develop a cold, rash or some form of discharge that means your system is going through a cleansing stage. Sometimes symptoms can appear to get worse for a short time – don't be alarmed as this is usually a sign that the remedy is taking effect, but always check with the homeopathic practitioner that this is a normal reaction.

greenfile

Certain substances, such as coffee, eucalyptus, menthol, spearmint and peppermint (including many proprietary toothpastes and mouthwashes, so use natural products), can neutralize homeopathic remedies and should be avoided.

The designation 6c or 30c after the name of a remedy refers to the amount of dilution. So, a 6c potency can be repeated more frequently.

WARNING Although over-the-counter remedies are available, you should never self-prescribe homeopathic treatment. In all cases, it is recommended that you contact a qualified homeopath for advice and treatment (see Useful Contacts, page 156).

In fact, if you have any response to the treatment that concerns you, contact your homeopath straight away. You may also want to make notes of any changes and take them with you to discuss at your next appointment.

The number of consultations required depends very much on the individual. Generally, acute conditions respond more quickly and the longer a chronic illness has existed, the longer it will take to disappear.

HOMEOPATHIC TREATMENT ON THE NHS
In the UK, you can ask your GP for a referral just as you would for any other hospital or specialist. Explain that you understand you are entitled to homeopathic treatment under the NHS. Depending on where you live, you will be referred to one of the Homeopathic Hospitals, a local NHS clinic, or a local doctor with homeopathic training. If your GP is resistant, explain your reasoning and stand your ground.

BENEFITS OF HOMEOPATHY
Pregnancy: There are remedies to treat minor health problems associated with pregnancy, such as mild urinary problems, diarrhoea, anaemia, varicose veins, backache and thrush, or emotional upset, and to help alleviate nausea and sickness, tiredness, cramps and heartburn. Homeopathy can be used to turn a breech baby, and to ensure that the labour and birth go smoothly by dealing with anxiety and fear and to tone the uterus.
Labour: Suitable remedies can help produce strong effective contractions, stimulate the uterus if it fails, and deal with exhaustion and irritability.
Post-natal mothers: Homeopathic remedies can aid a fast recovery from damage to delicate tissues, and from exhaustion and bruising. Homeopathy can also help establish a good flow of milk for breast-feeding mothers and help protect the nipples from cracking and soreness. It is also excellent for treating mastitis. There are specific remedies to help with baby blues and anxiety.

If you are given homeopathic remedies to take at a later date, be sure to store them in a cool dark place, away from anything with a strong smell. If you travel, do not let the remedies go through the X-ray machines at airports.

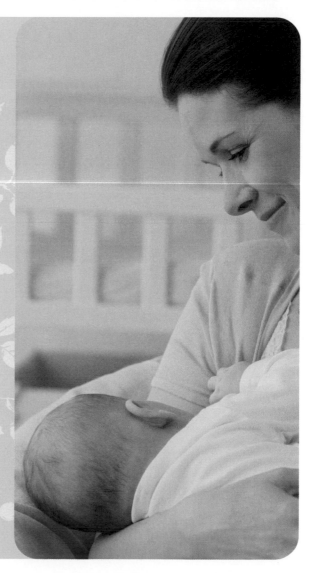

Shiatsu

Also known as Japanese 'finger pressure' therapy, shiatsu originates from the same oriental principles as acupuncture (see page 108) combined with a western knowledge of physiology.

Like acupressure, shiatsu works by manually stimulating the body's vital energy flow (known as ki in Japanese) in order to promote good health. However, in shiatsu, the practitioner uses thumbs and fingers, elbows and even knees and feet to apply pressure and stretching to the energy lines known as meridians.

Physically, this has the effect of stimulating the circulation and the flow of lymphatic fluid, working on both divisions of the autonomic nervous system, helping to release toxins and deep-seated tension from the muscles and stimulating the hormone system. On a subtler level, shiatsu allows you to relax deeply and get in touch with your body's healing abilities.

What to Expect at a Consultation

A personal case history will be recorded before the treatment. The *hara* is a very important diagnostic tool for shiatsu. For this, the practitioner will gently probe your abdomen to map the energetic state of your body, its organs and the corresponding meridians.

A shiatsu treatment is normally given on a padded mat at floor level or on a futon, while you lie, fully clothed, either prone, supine or on your side. You may also receive part of your treatment sitting in a chair or on the mat. The massage should be pleasurable and relaxing, not uncomfortable.

The practitioner may give advice on diet, exercise and lifestyle, encouraging self-understanding and greater independence in health matters. Your shiatsu practitioner may also offer you a personal health assessment. This will be an insight into your condition but does not constitute a medical diagnosis as such.

greenfile

You will get more from your treatment if you avoid eating a large meal, taking strenuous exercise or having a hot bath or shower just before or after a shiatsu treatment.

After shiatsu, you will probably feel invigorated yet relaxed. While patients generally experience increased well-being, there may be temporary healing reactions as toxins and negative emotions are released; these may take the form of a headache or flu-like symptoms for 24 hours. In such cases, contact your therapist.

Most practitioners recommend more than one shiatsu treatment to secure lasting improvement to health problems. A session lasts about 45 minutes.

BENEFITS OF SHIATSU

Pregnancy: Good for relieving morning sickness, vomiting and constipation, shiatsu is also commonly used to relieve headaches, neck and shoulder pain, back pain, sciatica, cramps, digestive problems, stress, fatigue and depression. In later pregnancy, it can help alleviate oedema, or swelling.

Labour: Can help to trigger labour if you are overdue, and can help to control pain.

Post-natal mothers: Helps with post-natal aches and pains, back and shoulder ache from breast-feeding and other common complaints.

WARNING Make sure your shiatsu practitioner has experience of working with pregnant women and knows to avoid certain acupoints during pregnancy. Always choose a qualified practitioner (see Useful Contacts, page 156).

Flower Remedies

It wasn't until as recently as the 1930s that German homeopath Edward Bach revived the ancient therapeutic use of flower remedies as first recorded by the ancient Egyptians. Perhaps his most well-known variety is the flower blend known as the Bach Rescue Remedy, which is often used for shock or panic, but which is also very good for calming the mind as the birth approaches.

Since the 1980s and the renaissance of complementary therapies, flower essences have grown in popularity, and now native plants from around the world, such as the Australian Bush remedies, are readily available in stores worldwide.

The therapeutic properties of the plants are harnessed by infusing them in spring water and preserving their essence in alcohol. Flower essences can be used to treat your emotional and spiritual state, but also physical conditions, as symptoms of ill-health are often considered a manifestation of problems on a higher or emotional level.

What to Expect at a Consultation

Flower remedy practitioners tend to work in their own specific ways. Many are intuitive healers who use dowsing to find the right combination of flower essences for you. Other practitioners rely on hearing a detailed account of your emotional and mental state and personality before prescribing a combination of essences to help you to deal with your situation.

Your practitioner may make up a bespoke remedy containing the prescribed essences for you, or you may be advised to buy the relevant individual essences. Both the made-up prescribed remedy and the individual essences are then diluted in mineral water or fruit juice, to be taken several times a day until the condition improves.

> **BENEFITS OF FLOWER ESSENCES**
>
> **Pregnancy:** Ideal for helping relieve emotional states, such as stress and anxiety, sleeplessness, depression and fear, or for physical complaints, such as pain or shock.
>
> **Labour:** Rescue Remedy is often used to calm the mind and ease pain and shock.
>
> **Post-natal mothers:** Flower essences are excellent for helping you deal with the spectrum of emotions that new mothers experience, ranging from exhaustion to feelings of overwhelming responsibility.

> **FLOWER ESSENCES FOR PREGNANCY AND BIRTH**
>
> Walnut, for adjustment to change
>
> Watermelon and courgette, for a harmonious pregnancy
>
> Mimulus, for fear of pain or things going wrong
>
> Rock rose, for terrifying thoughts
>
> Forget-me-not and Pineapple weed, for bonding with your baby
>
> Star of Bethlehem, for shock after a traumatic birth

WARNING Flower essences are safe to take through all stages of pregnancy but, since most are preserved in alcohol, it's important to follow dosage instructions carefully and not to exceed recommendations.

7 Health & Well-being

Pregnancy is the time in your life when you are forced to review your approach to health and healing. Given that many of the conventional medicines are no longer available to you, it is the perfect time to think about using a natural remedy to alleviate your health problems. This chapter looks at the common complaints you may experience during pregnancy and offers suggestions on ways to treat and relieve them naturally. You are still vulnerable to everyday illnesses, such as coughs and colds, and without recourse to conventional medicines it's good to know that there are some alternatives available. With the rush of hormones that accompanies pregnancy and the anxieties that may come and go, you may feel particularly vulnerable to your emotions, and there are therapies and remedies that can help you experience a positive pregnancy.

Natural medicine is gentle and effective. It will work with your body to deal with illness in the way that nature intended, without causing any harm to your unborn baby. No one is suggesting that you turn your back on conventional medicine. It has a valuable role to play in your antenatal care but very often you can successfully help and heal common ailments using tried-and-tested natural medicines without resorting to your doctor. This integrated approach to illness offers the best of all worlds.

NOTE The advice in this chapter should not be considered as a substitute for medical advice from your family doctor or any other qualified medical practitioner. If you treat yourself with natural medicines, such as herbs, you should always inform your doctor, because these can be very powerful and interact with prescribed or over-the-counter medications.

Common Pregnancy Complaints

There are a number of minor yet discomforting complaints that are common during pregnancy. You may be lucky and escape them but it's probably worth stocking up on a couple of basic natural ingredients that will help you to tackle the unpleasant side effects of conditions such as morning sickness, fatigue and cramps efficiently yet naturally.

Morning Sickness

Just over half of all pregnant women complain of morning sickness at some point in their pregnancy, most commonly during the first three months. Symptoms are often experienced on awaking in the morning, although morning sickness can strike at any time of the day or evening. Symptoms include nausea, vomiting, excessive salivation and a disinclination to eat.

Although morning sickness is unpleasant but mild for most women, some can be more seriously affected, becoming dehydrated and vitamin-deficient from excessive vomiting.

There is no definitive answer to what causes morning sickness and why some women get it while others don't. Theories include hormonal fluctuations, emotional reactions to pregnancy, nutritional factors and biological mechanisms that cause your body to reject substances that may cause the baby harm. Some believe that it's the body's way of eliminating toxins and that, as a result, those who suffer from morning sickness actually have a healthier pregnancy.

HOME-MADE GINGER TEA
Grate a 2.5-cm (1-in) length of peeled, fresh ginger root into a mug and pour on freshly boiled water. Leave to infuse for 5 minutes. Strain, add a squeeze of lemon and honey to taste, and sip slowly when cooled. Drink two or three times throughout the day to relieve symptoms.

What to do

The first course of action should be to avoid smells and foods that nauseate you (often spicy, gas-producing or fatty foods). Choose foods that appeal to you and regularly eat small, nutritious snacks, while drinking plenty of water to keep you hydrated.

Sipping herbal teas can offer relief from morning sickness. Ginger tea is the most common remedy (see above), but other herbal teas, such as chamomile, fennel, spearmint or peppermint, can be soothing and are able to relieve sickness.

Complementary therapies enjoy good results in the treatment of morning sickness (see page 100).

acupressure self-help
When feeling nauseous, press strongly with your thumb on the Pericardium 6 acupoint, which is located on the inside of your forearm at a point two thumb widths above the crease of the wrist and between the tendons.

greenfile
Keep a snack by your bed overnight so that you have something to eat before getting up in the morning. In my experience, a couple of ginger biscuits first thing did the trick.

Fatigue

Given the fact that your body is working overtime to help develop a new life inside, it's small wonder that you suddenly feel as if you have no energy. This is completely normal and you shouldn't be alarmed at all.

There are some sensible precautions you can take to help reduce the impact of this sudden fatigue, and some recommendations that may help you to sail through the acclimatization period while you adjust to the changes in your body and psyche.

What to do

To increase your energy levels, try boosting your diet with iron-rich foods together with foods high in vitamin C to help increase absorption (see page 44). Drinking nettle tea two or three times a day is another good way of boosting iron levels.

Make sure you are getting plenty of sleep. If you still feel tired, then take a nap. Learn to listen to your body and rest when you need to without worrying about the 'things that need doing'.

Conversely, taking a brisk walk in the fresh air is also an excellent way of increasing your oxygen intake and improving your circulation, so combating fatigue. In fact, any moderate exercise, inside or outside, can be invigorating and help to banish fatigue.

Don't be tempted to raise energy levels by snacking on energy-rich sugary foods, such as chocolate, or stimulants, such as coffee; this is a quick-fix, which will offer only temporary respite! By the same token, even herbal stimulants should be avoided during pregnancy. A better choice is to get some proper rest or nourishment and consider concentrated food supplements, such as spirulina and molasses (see page 59).

greenfile

A few drops of lemon, orange or sandalwood essential oil added to your morning bath can be invigorating and refreshing to both mind and spirit.

WARNING If you feel consistently exhausted and irritable, this could be an indication that you are anaemic. Consult your doctor or midwife for advice.

Heartburn

More than three-quarters of pregnant women suffer at some point from heartburn, a burning sensation in your chest and throat. Hormonal changes can soften the valve between the oesophagus and the stomach, allowing food and gastric juices to return into the oesophagus with the accompanying burning sensation or acute pain in the chest.

The situation is compounded as the pregnancy progresses and the growing baby puts pressure on the stomach, making symptoms worse in late pregnancy.

Heartburn often occurs after meals or as a result of eating the wrong foods but it can be alleviated by sensible eating and gentle soothing herbs.

What to do

Try eating frequent, smaller, low-fat meals to reduce the symptoms of heartburn. You should favour alkaline foods, such as fruits and vegetables, over acidic foods (see right) and try to avoid spicy, greasy and sugary foods. Some experts believe that a combination diet, for example eating proteins and carbohydrates separately and at different times of the day, can help to relieve heartburn.

It is also recommended that you eat a light evening meal earlier in the evening, say around 6 p.m., and have a small snack before going to bed, if required, rather than eating a large meal late in the evening.

Complementary therapies, such as acupuncture, reflexology, homeopathy, aromatherapy and herbalism, all report good results in the treatment of heartburn (see pages 100–117).

Sometimes lying down can aggravate heartburn, so sleep with an extra pillow(s) under your head.

greenfile

Slippery elm or dandelion teas are an excellent way to relieve the pain of heartburn. You can also take slippery elm lozenges.

ALKALINE AND ACIDIC FOODS

Most raw fruit and vegetables are alkalizing foods with the exceptions of cranberries, pomegranates, strawberries, plums, corn, broccoli and asparagus. Apple cider vinegar is alkalizing, while distilled white vinegar is acidifying. Almonds and chestnuts, and seeds, such as pumpkin, sunflower and flax, are considered to be alkaline foods. All herbal seasonings are considered to be alkalizing.

Nearly all cooking oils and all grains are considered to be acidifying foods, as are coffee and chocolate. Cheeses made from goat's and sheep's milk are acidifying foods, as are milk and butter. Most animal sources of foods, including tuna, shrimp, salmon and cottage cheese, are considered to be acid foods. All alcoholic beverages make the acid food list, as do any forms of pasta.

WARNING Avoid over-the-counter antacids and medicines, and even baking soda, which are contra-indicated during pregnancy.

Leg Cramps

Mildly painful leg cramps, often at night, are common during the second and third trimesters. They usually occur as a result of the extra weight that you are carrying, a lack of exercise or a calcium or magnesium deficiency.

Not all women experience leg cramps but rather have an uncomfortable, achy, restless or pulling sensation in their legs. These are simply milder symptoms of the same condition.

What to do

You can very easily reduce the frequency of leg cramps by taking a few simple remedial steps.

Firstly, try to build more activity into your daily routine and, at the same time, improve your mineral intake either by eating more calcium and magnesium in your diet (see pages 45 and 48) or by taking supplements. Vitamin E is also said to reduce cramping.

Often you can relieve a leg cramp by massaging and stretching your leg muscles. Flex and point your foot as you massage to release the tension.

Soak your feet and calves, if possible, in a warm footbath to which you have added a few drops of arnica.

Seventy-five per cent of pregnant women get stretch marks.

Skin Problems

Some women report that their skin improves thanks to the hormonal changes of pregnancy, but others are affected by itching and other skin troubles.

If you are eating a healthy, balanced diet, you may well avoid or reduce the discomfort of some of the more common skin problems. However, there are measures that you can take to alleviate many skin conditions.

What to do

Itchiness You may experience intense itchiness as the skin of your belly, breasts and thighs stretches. In addition, the liver is working harder to process the increased hormonal load and this can cause the skin to itch. Make sure your skin is well cleansed with mild natural soap or simply with clean, warm water. You can exfoliate with a loofah or soft body brush to stimulate circulation and leave the skin soft and clean. Moisturize well, using cocoa butter or vitamin E lotion. To reduce itching, use calendula oil or apply echinacea tincture mixed half-and-half with water.

greenfile

Lack of salt in your diet can cause muscle cramps, so although it is not normally necessary to salt your food, if you suffer from cramps, try sprinkling a little sea salt on your dinner.

CHLOASMA

Also known as the mask of pregnancy, chloasma is a darkening of the skin predominantly on the forehead, nose and cheeks below the eyes. This is not dangerous but can cause embarrassment for some women. Aloe vera gel is said to help lighten these areas during pregnancy but the darkened patches should return to their normal colour after childbirth.

WARNING After 28 weeks, if you experience severe, persistent itchy skin, consult your doctor as this could be an indication of obstetric cholestasis, a rare but serious condition that must be treated with conventional medicine.

Stretch marks These cannot necessarily be prevented but a diet rich in zinc, found in ginger, cheese and wholegrains, for example, is said to help. If the tell-tale silvery lines start to appear, you can nourish the area so they become less pronounced using vitamin E, almond or wheatgerm oil or herbal oils containing chamomile, mandarin, calendula or rose.

Sore Breasts

Even before you have confirmed that you are pregnant, you may experience tender, sore or tingly breasts with extremely sensitive nipples. This acute sensitivity usually subsides by the end of the first trimester but many women report that their breasts feel heavy and tender throughout the pregnancy due to their increased size. It is important to wear a supportive bra throughout your pregnancy (see page 80).

What to do

Soaking in a warm bath with the water covering your breasts can offer temporary relief from discomfort and heaviness. You can alleviate tenderness in early pregnancy by massaging your breasts once or twice a day with a soothing herbal oil. Try mixing several drops of rose geranium or arnica essential oils into a base oil of sweet almond (3 oz) for a soothing, scented massage oil.

Swelling

Mild swelling, or oedema, particularly of the feet and ankles, is quite normal during pregnancy, especially towards the latter stages. Hot weather, prolonged standing or fatigue can all aggravate the situation.

Normal swelling should reduce after you rest and in the morning when you wake up.

What to do

Preventive measures are best when dealing with oedema. Make sure you raise your feet when sitting for about 20 minutes, three or four times a day. If possible, periodically lie down with your feet above your heart level to help circulation. Similarly, you should avoid standing for extended periods, especially in hot weather.

Regular exercise enhances circulation and helps to avoid or reduce swelling.

When sleeping, try to lie on your left side to improve circulatory function.

Constipation

Virtually all women, especially those who are overweight, experience constipation during pregnancy because the hormone progesterone slows bowel movements. To add insult to injury, the combination of constipation together with increased rectal pressure due to the weight of the baby puts you at risk of haemorrhoids.

As with most ailments, prevention is better than cure, so a few adjustments to your daily routine may help you to avoid this uncomfortable condition that is the root cause of so many other pregnancy complaints, including indigestion, headaches and skin problems.

What to do

The most common cure for constipation is to use laxatives. However, you should avoid over-the-counter

WARNING The medical term for swelling is oedema. However, if after you press your finger onto your legs or hands, you leave an indentation mark, this is called pitting oedema, which may indicate a more serious condition. You should seek advice from your doctor in this case.

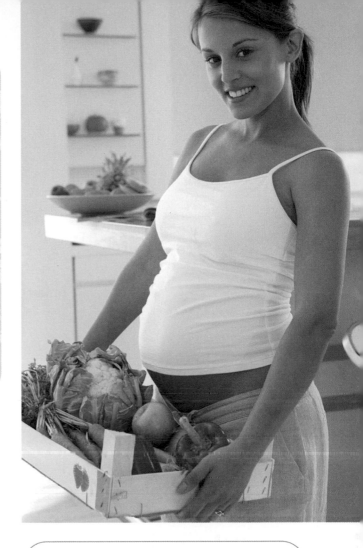

CONSTIPATION: PREVENTIVE MEASURES

Increase your physical activity – exercise helps to stimulate the muscle contractions in the colon.

Drink lots of water.

Drink a cup of hot water with a dash of lemon before breakfast.

Limit processed foods and caffeinated beverages.

Eat beets and cabbage – these are a gentle laxative.

Eat lots of fresh fruit and vegetables (at least some raw).

Give yourself time each day to sit on the toilet, relax and wait

Do not ignore your body's signal to empty your bowels – go to the toilet without delay.

To alleviate the pain of haemorrhoids, a traditional cure is to put grated potato or carrot directly on the affected area.

laxatives in favour of a mild natural laxative (although milk of magnesia is safe during pregnancy).

The most effective natural laxative that is safe during pregnancy is dandelion root tincture, which is available from health food shops and natural pharmacies.

A popular Ayurvedic (traditional Indian medicine) remedy for constipation is to drink a mug of hot milk mixed with a teaspoon of ghee (clarified butter) at bedtime.

You can also massage your abdomen to help stimulate bowel movement. You should recline on a bed, sofa or even in a warm bath. Massage your abdomen quite deeply in a circular, clockwise direction, for about ten minutes. Then proceed to the toilet.

Some complementary therapies, such as acupuncture, homeopathy, herbalism and nutritional therapy, are successful in the treatment of constipation and haemorrhoids (see pages 100–117).

WARNING Herbal laxatives such as castor oil, senna, buckthorn and aloes should be avoided during pregnancy.

greenfile

Physiologically speaking, squatting is the best position for bowel movements. Strange as it may seem, actually squatting on the toilet seat – while exercising extreme caution – or sitting with your feet raised on a stool, or even tip-toe, can assist the process.

For some women, eating bran (an excellent remedy for constipation, in fact) can irritate the intestine lining. Oats are a less aggravating alternative, especially when cooked with raisins, so why not have a bowl of porridge to start the day?

Everyday Ailments

Before your pregnancy, everyday aches and pains or the symptoms of coughs and colds could be dealt with by the contents of your medicine cabinet. During your pregnancy, these conventional medicines or painkillers may be unsuitable and you will need to find natural alternatives to ensure that you and your baby maintain a healthy, drug-free pregnancy.

Back Pain

Many pregnant women get backache for numerous reasons but if you suffered with back problems before your pregnancy, it is even more likely that you will get bouts of backache at this time.

The weight of your growing baby places a great deal of stress on your lower back muscles, and this can then be compounded by poor posture. In addition, urinary tract infections (see page 128) and constipation (see page 124) are common during pregnancy and these can, in turn, lead to backache.

What to do

Any of the postural body work therapies, such as Alexander technique, yoga, qi gong and polarity therapy, are useful to correct your posture if backache is persistent.

If you can't attend a class, then try to improve your posture yourself: avoid the habit of swaying your back to accommodate the weight at the front. Rather, stand up straight, tuck your tailbone under so that your pelvis is not tilting forward and let your shoulder blades drop down your back. Try to correct yourself

greenfile

You can make an effective, warming poultice by mixing two cups of white breadcrumbs with a tablespoon of cayenne pepper and enough warm water to make a dough-like consistency.

Position this on the affected area of your lower back, but do not leave on for more than 15–20 minutes as the cayenne may burn the skin.

to this posture whenever you catch yourself slipping back into bad habits. (There is actually a medical term for the swayed back, belly out position adopted by many pregnant women – it's called lordosis.)

Osteopathy and chiropractic are the best-known complementary therapies for back pain, but shiatsu and acupuncture are also recognized as being highly beneficial at bringing relief from the pain and discomfort of backache and sciatica (see pages 100–117).

Massage is also very helpful (see page 38). Obviously, a professional massage can help but even if your partner or friend simply rubs your back using a little warm, gentle massage oil, this can help to give respite from the discomfort.

Remember to rest and take the weight off your feet (and pelvis) as often as you can with your feet up. Applying heat to the affected area (wrap a hot water bottle in a towel or use a wheat bag) can sometimes help. Following the same principle, soaking in a hot bath is also recommended.

SCIATICA
Sciatica is the medical term for a pain that travels from the lower back down the back of the leg, through the calf and to the outer aspect of the foot. It is caused by inflammation of the sciatic nerve, and is common in women in the later months of pregnancy.

Colds and Flu

Although a common cold or influenza can be extremely debilitating during pregnancy, it should not be a threat to you or your baby. However, if you have a prolonged fever or high fever, then you should consult your GP. Otherwise, it's a case of making sure you get plenty of rest, eating highly nutritious and natural foods and waiting it out while you treat the symptoms with natural cures.

On a cautionary note, if you have used herbs to treat a cold or flu when you were not pregnant, you may have to review your usual treatments, since some herbs are not safe for use during pregnancy. These are the ones also used in some aromatherapy oils (see page 38).

What to do

It is important that you remember to drink lots of fluids when you have a cold or flu, even if you don't really feel like it. If you become dehydrated, your kidneys will become over-taxed and your baby could be adversely affected. So, as a general rule of thumb, you need to drink a cup of water, diluted juice or herbal or fruit tea at least every two hours – more if you're feverish.

At the first signs of a cold, many women swear by the use of echinacea root tincture to reduce the symptoms and to limit the duration of the cold. There have been some concerns raised about the safety of echinacea during pregnancy, but to date, the evidence suggests that there is no increased risk of birth defects or other pregnancy related health problems.

Sipping fruit or herbal teas can be effective for reducing the fever, aches and discomfort of a common cold or flu. Try lemon balm, chamomile or elderflower and, in moderation, ginger or dried yarrow. However, do not take yarrow during the first trimester.

Garlic is a natural bactericide and therefore useful in the treatment of many common ailments, including colds and sore throats. Taken in conjunction with vitamin C, it is particularly potent.

Cystitis

Also known as Urinary Tract Infections (UTIs), cystitis is a common complaint that can affect you at any time, but it is particularly widespread during pregnancy because the weight of the womb upon the bladder and ureters increases the likelihood of stasis (a stagnation in the normal flow), which breeds bacteria and can lead to infection.

Symptoms include frequent urination (sometimes hard to distinguish from the greater frequency brought on by pregnancy), often accompanied by burning sensation or pain on passing water. In some cases,

WARNING You should avoid sexual intercourse if you have cystitis.

NATURAL COLD REMEDY

A German friend gave me this recipe when I was pregnant with my first child and I've used it for the relief of colds and sore throats ever since.

½ onion, sliced

2 cloves of garlic, chopped

1.5-cm (½-in) piece of ginger root, chopped or grated

1 tablespoon olive oil

Sugar or honey, to taste

In a small pan, sauté the onion, garlic and ginger together in the oil. Cover with cold water and bring to the boil. Reduce to a simmer and then add sugar or honey to sweeten. Strain and sip when cooled.

you may also experience flu-like symptoms, tenderness above the pubic bone and, very rarely, vaginal bleeding.

Cystitis responds well to natural treatments but if left untreated, it can become much more serious and develop into a kidney infection. This can be a serious threat to your health, and immediate attention from your doctor is required.

What to do

To ease cystitis, you should listen to the old wives' tale and drink cranberry juice. Now scientifically proven, it's known that cranberries prevent pathogenic bacteria from adhering to the wall of the bladder. If you can't get hold of fresh cranberries to make your own juice or smoothies, the best alterantive is to buy organic, pure cranberry juice (which you may have to sweeten) rather than the artificially sweetened commercial brands.

As well as cranberry juice, you should drink as much water as possible during the day to help flush the system.

If urinating is extremely painful, then pour warm water over the entrance to the urethra as you sit on the toilet. Alternatively, urinate in a shallow bath (making sure to clean the bath well afterwards). A warm bath with a couple of drops of chamomile, geranium or lavender essential oils may ease cystitis symptoms.

greenfile

Avoid eating beetroot, tomatoes and citrus fruits when suffering from cystitis as these are likely to aggravate the condition.

A reflexologist (see page 105) can stimulate the kidney, bladder and urinary tract reflex points on the foot to try to disperse the toxins that are causing cystitis, so it may be worthwhile consulting one if the cystitis returns.

Headache

Normally, when you get a headache, you may take a couple of pain killers and continue with your day as usual. However, when you're pregnant, you cannot take your normal pain relief medication. During pregnancy, when you get a headache – and ten per cent of pregnant women suffer from more severe headaches or migraine – you have to rely on natural remedies, which can be just as effective.

What to do

Firstly, you should try to identify what is causing your headache. Is it linked to the hormonal changes that occur in pregnancy? Is it perhaps caused by stress or tension in the muscles of the head and neck due to poor posture? Is it a migraine triggered by something you may have eaten or done?

Sometimes, getting some fresh air and taking a little exercise at the same time – perhaps a walk in the park, for example – is enough to lift a headache or to stop it developing.

Again, as with many of these everyday ailments, making sure you're getting enough sleep and rest is essential, and try to reduce stress levels if you think tension is the root cause of your headaches. You might like to try the meditation and relaxation techniques outlined on pages 36–9, as they are particularly good at relaxing tight muscles and relieving tension.

Some traditional midwives recommend taking a brief hot shower followed immediately by a quick blast of cold shower to relieve a headache, but it's not for the faint-hearted. Often, a headache can be relieved by stimulating certain acupoints on the face and head.

SELF-MASSAGE TO RELIEVE MIGRAINE HEADACHES

Place the fingers of both hands on either side of the midline of the back of your neck, just under the base of the skull.

With elbows raised and fingers perpendicular to the neck's midline, apply pressure to your neck muscles with your finger tips.

Sweep up the neck, deeply massaging the neck muscles, and then back down the neck, massaging as you go.

Try using your thumb to apply gentle pressure to the point between your eyebrows, just above the bridge of your nose. You can also massage the part of the head that is hurting, using a gentle circular movement. You or a partner can extend the massage down the neck and shoulders to ease muscle tension and improve blood circulation.

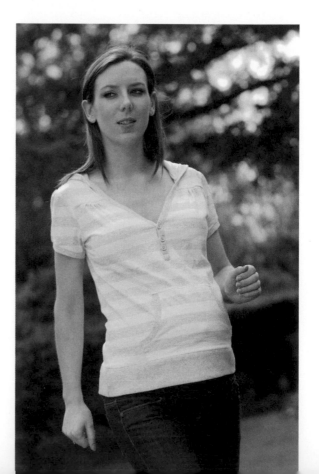

greenfile

Headaches are commonly caused in pregnancy by dehydration or low blood sugar levels. Drink plenty of water and always have a healthy snack with you.

Try putting 3–4 drops of lavender oil on a compress and applying to the temples to relieve a headache.

Sore or Bleeding Gums

Changes in oestrogen and progesterone levels can cause your gums to become inflamed, resulting in them bleeding when you brush or floss your teeth. In severe cases you can develop gingivitis, which often worsens as your pregnancy progresses. You should consult your GP or dentist if you suspect you have gingivitis as, if left untreated, it can cause serious gum and bone problems.

What to do

You can soothe sore or bleeding gums, which are common in the first half of pregnancy, by sipping chamomile tea or by rinsing the mouth with a chamomile infusion (see right).

A diet rich in vitamin C can help to prevent gum problems. Good vitamin C food choices include apricots, blackcurrants, citrus fruits, apples, cherries, watercress, Brussels sprouts and alfalfa.

In addition, the homeopathic remedies Kreosotum 6c and Phosphorus 6c are said to be effective for the relief of inflamed, swollen or bleeding gums – seek advice from a trained homeopath (see page 114).

Carpal Tunnel Syndrome

This condition is caused by swelling in the hands that restricts nerves in the wrist. It is particularly common in the third trimester. You may experience numb, tingling or painful fingers, often worse at night.

What to do

Acupuncture, shiatsu, homeopathy and osteopathy (see pages 108, 116, 114, 103) are all useful therapies for treating carpal tunnel syndrome and a physiotherapist can provide splints to support the wrists. However, you can also follow some self-help techniques to ease this painful condition. Try gently circling and flexing the wrists in cold water to reduce swelling and pressure on the nerves in the wrist. To stretch the carpal tunnel, crouch down and gently press the palms of the hands flat on the floor.

When you rest, make sure you elevate your hands and forearms on pillows and take extra care when handling hot liquids, especially when you first wake up and the symptoms and numbness are at their worst.

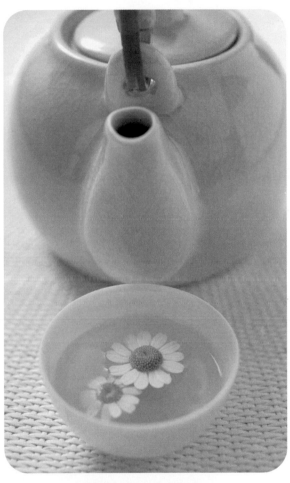

CHAMOMILE MOUTHWASH
Infuse 2 teaspoons of chamomile in freshly boiled water for 10 minutes, strain, cool and rinse around mouth for a minute before spitting out.

WARNING If you have severe swelling that doesn't go down together with a headache, contact your doctor or midwife as this could be a sign of pre-eclampsia.

Emotional Issues

Pregnancy is one of the greatest changes that you are likely to undergo in your life. As well as all the physical transformations taking place, there are many changing factors in your life that can affect you emotionally and may cause you to feel anxious or depressed or to have sleepless nights.

Anxiety

Whether this is your first or your fourth pregnancy, it is only natural to worry. What's important is that you don't allow natural concerns that can motivate you to have the best, healthiest and most natural pregnancy possible, to turn in to fruitless and negative anxiety.

If you find that you are anxious a good deal of the time, then you should use some of the relaxation techniques on pages 36–9, while eating a nutritious, healthy diet (see pages 42–63) and getting plenty of exercise.

Talking to your friends and partner about your concerns and/or joining an antenatal childbirth class can help to allay your worries. However, if you still feel anxious, then some of the following natural remedies may well help.

What to do

When you are anxious, you hold your breath and your chest is tight. Take your mind off your worries by focusing on your breathing. As you breathe in, slow your breath to the count of three, then slowly breathe out to the count of four. Repeat this exercise until you feel your body and your ribcage start to relax. You can accentuate the calming effects of this breathing exercise if you visualize your in-breath as a vivid blue colour, and the out-breath as a glittering gold. You'll find that as you relax and breathe more deeply, the breathing will move from shallow breaths in your upper chest through lower chest and then to the belly, giving your body the rich oxygen it needs.

As you feel your levels of anxiety rising, take a couple of drops of the Bach Rescue Remedy to help you relax. Alternatively, a couple of drops of chamomile, lavender, rose, mandarin or sandalwood essential oil in a warm bath can be very soothing.

Drinking calming herbal teas, such as chamomile or lemon balm, throughout the day can also help to keep anxiety at bay.

Sleeplessness

Despite feeling completely shattered, perversely, many pregnant women experience difficulties with getting to sleep, or if they are disturbed in the night by the baby's movements or because they have to go to the toilet, they then find it hard to get back to sleep. However, adequate sleep and rest are important if you are to be ready to cope with the demands of a new baby.

What to do

Before bedtime, create an environment that is conducive to sleep. So avoid stimulating activities, such as the computer, telephone calls or hectic television shows. Instead, turn to quieter more relaxing activities, such as reading, taking a candle-lit bath (add a couple of drops of lavender oil) or listening to relaxing music. Make sure that you are not so relaxed

greenfile

Consider hypnotherapy or counselling if your anxiety levels are ruining the enjoyment of your baby's imminent arrival.

WARNING A certain amount of anxiety during pregnancy is natural, but if you suspect that your levels of stress and anxiety are adversely affecting you or your baby, or if depression persists, talk to your midwife or doctor.

in the bath that you fall asleep, and always take fire safety precautions if using candles.

The common tradition of having a hot milky drink at bedtime is based on scientific fact. Milk contains calcium, which helps to combat insomnia and relax muscles. So a cup of warm milk with a sprinkling of cinnamon added can be very beneficial if taken just before you retire for the night. If you're not fond of cow's milk, then chamomile, passionflower or lime blossom herbal tea as a bedtime drink can be effective in helping you to fall asleep.

Depression

There are many reasons why you may have odd moments of depression while pregnant, even if you do not suffer from the condition at other times. Firstly, you probably realize that hormonal changes can affect both your physical and emotional state, but did you know that depression can result from nutritional deficiencies and dehydration as well as the more obvious emotional upset caused by the re-emergence of old fears and new concerns about coping? Nutritional deficiencies and dehydration can be easily avoided or rectified by following a healthy-eating regime and drinking plenty of water. Emotional causes of depression can be helped by an holistic approach.

What to do

Numerous studies have shown that regular exercise reduces the number of depressive episodes and anxiety attacks and increases emotional stability. So get out there doing whichever activity appeals most, whether it's swimming, walking, yoga, tai chi or ballroom dancing!

When you're depressed, you breathe six times faster than when you're not, so if you're feeling low, try the breathing exercises for calming anxiety (see page 132).

Massage is proven to alleviate depression as it stimulates the release of the body's natural pain killers (endorphins) and reduces levels of the stress hormones, cortisol and noradrenaline. A regular massage, or even a back and shoulder rub by your partner, can be relaxing and a great foil against depression.

Certain essential oils work very quickly on your nervous system and can be effective against temporary episodes of depression. Orange blossom, mandarin, grapefruit, rose and lavender oils are all effective. Use a couple of drops of oil added to a bath, in a vaporizer or blended with a carrier oil for aromatherapy massage. Complementary therapies such as flower essences, herbalism, reiki, acupuncture, hypnotherapy and homeopathy all report good results for treating depression. Also consult a nutritionist as nutritional deficiencies are often a cause of hormonal imbalance.

greenfile

Although governmental agencies and conventional health professionals have approved the artificial sweetener, aspartame, as safe for pregnant women, many holistic practitioners advise that women avoid it during pregnancy because it is linked to food allergies, sensitivities and depression. Check food and drink labels – aspartame is widely used in diet colas and low-sugar or low-calorie foods.

Natural Birth Options

You have come all the way through your pregnancy choosing the greener, more natural options for you and your baby. Now, as you near the date for the birth, and the start of a new phase in your life, it's time to make some important decisions about the type of birthing experience that you would most like to have.

Certainly, there is no right or wrong way to give birth. At home? In hospital? With or without pain relief? These are the sorts of questions that will be running through your mind as you approach full-term, yet only you can know what feels right for you. However, if you acquaint yourself fully with all the birthing options available to you, you stand a better chance of choosing the setting and style that best resonates with you and your beliefs.

The following pages give you the low-down on what to expect when you go into labour (see page 136), so you can start to form an idea about whether you might want a home birth (see page 140). If you veer towards a hospital birth, there are ways to make the experience as green and natural as possible and to avoid many of the routine medical interventions (see pages 143–6).

Finally, let's look slightly further ahead. We'll assume that you've had a wonderful birth experience and that you and your new family are settling back in to life at home. A few tips about those early post-partum days may prove useful (see page 152).

Childbirth

By the end of a pregnancy most mothers are eagerly anticipating the arrival of their baby, but very few look forward to the labour. In part, this is because the unknown is always frightening and, irrespective of whether it's your first or your fourth child, every delivery is different.

Nonetheless, while no one can really prepare you for what you are about to experience, if you have prepared well for the birth and have a relaxed and positive approach, you will fare better than if you are over-tired or anxious.

During your antenatal care you should have been encouraged to think about the kind of birth experience you would like and even to formulate a birth plan (see page 89). By the same token, you should also have been warned that things do not always go to plan and that you have the right to change your mind.

Women who have very set ideas about how their birth will progress can feel that they have let themselves down if things do not go according to plan. This is a great shame and such unyielding views put an unrealistic burden upon the mother (and baby).

There is no wrong or right way to have a baby. As long as the baby is not put at any risk, you do whatever you have to do to get through the birth the best way possible. In recent years, there has been something of a volte-face in delivery rooms, with natural births winning the labour laurels while those wanting an epidural are seen as wimps.

In truth, as long as your baby is safe, there is no extra merit in giving birth without pain relief unless it is what you truly want to do.

If you find the labour very painful or unbearable, don't feel afraid to ask for pain relief. You have not failed in any way and there is no shame attached. After all, it is not a competition. Yet, for those who prefer to experience the whole birthing process naturally, I can vouch that it is a wondrous experience. None of us knows how we are going to react in the face of pain and the unknown, so just keep an open mind.

Giving Birth

Labour is usually classified into three stages. How long it takes from start to finish varies considerably from individual to individual and, in the main, there is very little that you can do to affect the duration of the birth. It has to be said that a fit, relaxed and healthy woman tends to have an easier time of it, simply because she has more stamina and physical resources to draw upon. However, sometimes, the most slothful of women deliver in a matter of minutes while the athlete finds herself pushing hours later. There is no rhyme or reason for it. Nonetheless, whatever the duration of labour, we all follow the same stages of the process.

First Stage: Labour

Early labour stage This is when the cervix softens and starts to dilate to the first 4 cm (1½ in). You may have a 'show' during this stage (the name given to the plug of bloody mucus that was guarding the entrance of the cervix). Some women's waters break before or during the first part of labour and these fluids (from the amniotic sac) serve as a useful lubrication. Don't worry if your waters don't break at the outset, they will go in good

---

greenfile

Do what feels natural and comfortable to you. However, correct breathing, walking, kneeling, standing or sitting in different positions are all known to help to ease the pain of contractions. Try to relax fully between contractions and take lots of fluids – sports drinks and fruit juices if allowed, otherwise water and/or ice cubes.

LABOUR BAG FOR HOSPITAL

Have your bag ready from around 36 weeks, just in case you need to head out of the door in a hurry!

Clothes for you during labour and after birth, including bathrobe and nursing bra, slippers and socks (your feet can get cold during labour)

Clothes for baby (including a babygrow or sleepsuit, socks, blanket, hat, outdoor clothes to travel home) and nappies

Toiletries, including moisturizer, lip balm containing aloe vera and vitamin E and massage oil

Hair bands or scrunchies, if appropriate

Hot water bottle or wheat bag

Hand mirror for watching head crowning

Approved flower essences, aromatherapy oils or homeopathic remedies

Scented candles and relaxing music

Tens machine, with batteries, if appropriate (see page 147)

Food for you and your birth partner

Camera/camcorder and list of telephone numbers of friends

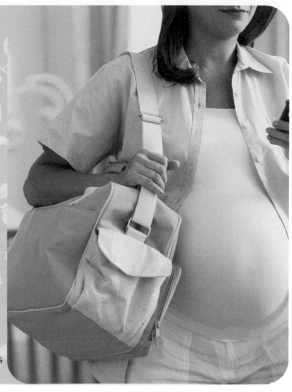

time. The midwife may offer to rupture the membrane artificially for you – this is your choice (see page 143).

At the beginning, contractions can be 10–20 minutes apart, lasting up to 30 seconds, or they may be every five minutes and lasting a minute or more. Although it may seem like no small achievement to you, sad to say, it is still called the early labour, or sometimes learn-to-labour, phase.

PROGRESS CHECK

To check how far you have progressed in your labour, the midwife will insert her fingers into your vagina to check the softness (effacement) and openness (dilation) of the cervix. This examination should not be painful although many women report discomfort.

During the early (latent) stage of labour you may dilate up to 4 cm (1½ in), during the active stage from 4–7 cm (1½–2¾ in), and during transition you will dilate from 7–10 cm (2¾–4 in). Once fully dilated, the baby is ready to be born.

Before you head to the hospital (when contractions are 3–4 minutes apart, although you should be guided by your care giver), you can help to ease contractions by walking around or taking a warm bath.

Active or hard labour starts once you've passed the 4 cm (1½ in) dilation point. During this phase, your baby descends further into the pelvis and you become fully dilated (10cm/4in).

You should now be doing the breathing and relaxation exercises that you learnt at your antenatal classes. However, I hesitate to say that you 'should' be doing anything since, although midwives and care givers report that this works to good effect, you are master of your own destiny at this point and 'should' really doesn't come into it.

Transition Dilation from 4 to 10 cm (1½ to 4 in) can take a matter of minutes or hours. For many women, this is the hardest part of the delivery. It's known as the transition, or advanced active, phase of labour.

Your uterus does 80–85 per cent of the actual work of expelling your baby; your pushing adds the crucial remaining 15 per cent.

Contractions are intensely painful and seem interminable. At the end of this stage, you may experience a lot of pressure against your lower back, perineum and rectum and the desire to push down and expel the baby is at its strongest.

At this point, some women, myself included, experience a serene moment of tranquillity, akin to the calm before the storm, as the body prepares itself for the big push.

Second Stage: Delivery

Pushing You may get a renewed burst of energy at this point in your labour or you may simply feel exhausted

BIRTHING POSITIONS

No longer are women expected to lie on their back on a bed to deliver a baby. There are many options available now, both for a home and hospital delivery. Getting into the best position during labour and birth can speed up the process considerably and make you more comfortable throughout. Why not try:

Kneeling on hands and knees

Sitting or reclining (on a birthing stool, the toilet, a birthing ball or reclining against the side of a bed or birth rail)

Squatting (supported or free-standing)

Upright or standing

Side-lying (particularly beneficial for resting during a long labour)

Keeping your mouth and jaw relaxed during breathing helps to keep your vaginal muscles relaxed, too.

and just want the whole palaver over and done with. Unfortunately, whatever your feelings, you have no choice but to work quite hard now.

Once you feel pushing urges, your baby should be born within a couple of hours. Second-time mothers may even deliver their baby within ten minutes of feeling the urge to push.

As you push with each contraction, you'll feel the baby move forward and then slide back a little. Don't be discouraged – it's quite natural and in fact good for the baby and your expanding vagina.

Crowning As the head starts to crown (when the widest part of the head is still visible after a contraction ends), you'll experience extreme pressure in your bottom, often described as a burning feeling, and many women report a sensation of tearing at the perineum. This is rarely the case and the midwife will be applying pressure to the area to reduce the risk of tears or need for an episiotomy (see page 145).

Delivery As your baby's head emerges, you may well feel a burning sensation in your vagina and you may be told to stop pushing at this point to avoid tearing. Once the head is out, your baby will turn to one side, the shoulders will come out and, finally, the rest of the body will follow. The relief and elation are immense.

Holding your baby What happens next varies depending on where you have your baby and your personal preferences. Sometimes, the baby is placed on your abdomen directly after the birth. On other occasions, the baby is checked and wrapped before being placed in your arms. The midwife will assess your baby using the Apgar scale (see page 141).

Third Stage: Delivering the Placenta

At some point shortly after your baby has been born, you will be asked to expel the placenta. As your midwife places a hand on your abdomen, she'll ask you to push again. You may feel slight cramps, but the euphoria at having your baby usually tempers this.

It is important that your uterus contracts at this stage to minimize bleeding. If your care giver suspects you're losing too much blood, she may massage your abdomen vigorously to encourage the uterus to contract or you may be given an injection that has the same effect.

AFTER PAINS

After pains are the name given to contractions that occur after you have given birth. They are caused by your uterus shrinking back down to its pre-pregnancy size and shape, which usually takes around 15 days.

After pains are not a cause for concern but they can cause discomfort or even pain. Although some women are not affected, those who are notice that contractions are most intense in the first few days after giving birth. You may also notice them more when you breast-feed. This happens because the uterus is still sensitive to the oxytocin released while nursing.

Some believe that after pains are negligible with a first baby and that they increase after each subsequent baby, although this is not always the case.

Comfort measures include placing warm packs or a hot-water bottle on your abdomen, gently massaging your abdomen and visualizing a stream of energy flowing through your uterus, down your legs to your toes.

If after pains are persistently severe after a week or so, consult your midwife or doctor to eliminate any other problems, such as infection.

Home Births

It comes as no surprise that women have been having babies at home for centuries. What's less well known is that research now shows that if you are a low-risk pregnant woman attended by a trained care giver, then home births are perfectly safe today. In fact, some advocates of home birth would argue that home births are safer in terms of the lowered risk of infection, the need for intervention and maternal haemorrhaging.

So, if you have a loving and safe home environment and your health team evaluate you as a low-risk pregnancy, then this could be the most natural option for you. Unfortunately, if you are expecting twins, your baby is in the breech position or you're a first-time mother aged over 35, your doctor/midwife team are less likely to sanction a home birth, although it's not impossible to proceed.

However, one important consideration to take into account when making a decision about a home birth is how close the hospital facilities are, just in case something were to go wrong and you need to be transferred for an emergency Caesarean delivery or resuscitation of the baby. If you live a long way from medical facilities, this could influence your decision to have a home birth and it may also affect the agreement of your attending midwife.

These risks have to be weighed against the undoubted benefits of being relaxed and comfortable in your own home environment with your loved ones (and possibly children) around you – what could be more natural!

Labour and Birth

Let us assume that you fit all the criteria and you're having your baby at home. You should have all the necessary supplies that your midwife has recommended on hand when your labour starts. Your midwife will join you at your home once the contractions are approximately 3–4 minutes apart. She will probably encourage you to walk and stand

GREEN GOODY BAG

Make sure you have readily to hand a selection of your favourite green goodies. Suggestions include:

Hot-water bottle or wheat bag

Ice cubes

Lip balm (containing aloe vera and vitamin E)

Hand mirror for watching head crowning

Massage oil

Approved flower essences and aromatherapy oils

Approved botanical/herbal or homeopathic remedies

Scented candles

Relaxing music

Bean bag

Warm socks

Birth ball, stool or pool, if appropriate

Tens machine, with batteries, if appropriate (see page 147)

as much as possible to increase dilation. She will regularly check your dilation, effacement, urine, blood pressure, pulse and temperature. She will also listen to the baby's heart rate using a Doppler stethoscope or a fetoscope (trumpet).

Apart from these periodic checks, you are free to move around, assume any position that's comfortable or rest as you wish. If you have had a birthing pool set up at home, you may spend as much time in the water as you like. You can use approved herbal tinctures, acupressure, flower essences, homeopathic remedies, massage, candles, music and supplements to your heart's content – your midwife may well encourage this. Some midwives are even trained in providing holistic remedies to help ease the pain and speed up labour.

Your partner, friends or relatives who are with you are at liberty to be as involved as they want to be, or as much as feels right for you. A massage from your partner can be hugely relaxing and beneficial, as can a cool cloth wiped over your face. Sometimes, standing with your arms around your partner's neck and pushing down can be helpful and it, too, is very inclusive.

Unless there are signs that your baby is becoming distressed, or the labour is progressing very slowly, you will be encouraged to push only when you feel like it. Home-birth midwives often suggest that you try pushing while bent over on your hands and knees. This is a comfortable position and can sometimes speed up labour. Others may bring a birthing stool for you to try.

A trained care giver may offer you a perineal massage when the baby's head is resting on the perineal floor. Some believe this reduces the need for an episiotomy. As the head crowns (see page 138), you might like to ask if someone can hold a mirror for you so you can see the first glimpse of your new baby.

As soon as the baby is born, she will be placed on your abdomen or chest. Some midwives suction the baby's nose and mouth and dry her before passing her to you. Your partner may well be invited to cut the baby's cord. The baby is assessed using the Apgar scale (see below).

THE APGAR TEST
This test, given by the midwife, assesses the health of your newborn baby at one and five minutes after the birth.

It checks your baby's Appearance, Pulse, Grimace, Activity and Respiration.

<table>
<tr><td>

greenfile

Your midwife may use nipple stimulation to speed up your labour. A hot shower may also be suggested.

Women who deliver their baby at home rarely require suturing (stitches).

</td></tr>
</table>

After the Birth

At a home birth, the midwife prefers the placenta to be expelled naturally and this can take anywhere up to an hour. The baby will probably be put to your breast as this stimulates the nipples, which in turn increases uterine contractions and so helps to expel the placenta. The midwife may also strongly massage your abdomen to encourage its expulsion. If, however, there is no sign of the placenta separating, you will be given an injection to make this happen.

Once the placenta has been checked to make sure it is intact and you have been examined for tears and lacerations and treated if necessary, you will then be left alone with your new baby and your partner, friends or family. This is a wonderful moment that you will cherish for a lifetime.

About an hour or so later, the midwife will return to give your baby a vitamin K injection, if agreed, or oral medication if not. In the US, your baby will also receive eye drops immediately after the birth to prevent any eye infections. The midwife will complete a neonatal examination of your baby and also check on your progress. You are then left in peace in the comfort of your own home with your new family, but you can, of course, call your midwifery team at

THE PLACENTA – YOUR OPTIONS
After checking the placenta is intact, the midwife will seal it in a plastic bag and take it away to dispose of it, usually by incineration. If you wish, you can keep the placenta to dispose of yourself (although it is illegal to throw it in the refuse in the US).

any time if you have any concerns or worries, either about yourself or your baby.

Most mothers who retain their placenta for disposal choose to bury it (or 'plant' it) in the garden. It's even been known for mothers to put coloured inks on it and to take a print – one mother told me that with the umbilical cord hanging down, the print looked like the tree of life. Occasionally, women choose to eat the placenta (most often fried in butter but occasionally raw) to get the nutrients.

If you choose to dispose of your placenta yourself, it is perfectly safe to keep it in the freezer while you decide what you'd like to do.

Greener Birth Options

Since you have chosen to read this book, it is highly likely that you have followed a natural, green and optimum health approach to your pregnancy, which is sure to offer your baby the very best start in life.

Nonetheless, as you reach the last weeks of your pregnancy, despite your best efforts to date, certain unavoidable circumstances could increase the chances of medical intervention during the birth. Should you find yourself in one of these out-of-the-ordinary situations, here are some natural suggestions for averting the need for medical help.

Breech Position

If your baby is in a breech position (head under your ribs and bottom in your pelvis), after 34–36 weeks, there is a good chance that your medical team will suggest a Caesarean delivery. Vaginal breech deliveries are rarely offered for breech babies now, but if your baby is not successfully turned and you want a vaginal delivery, it would be sensible to discuss this with your obstetrician, doctor or midwife, who can advise on the availability of delivery staff who have appropriate experience. Some doctors advise an epidural for every woman having a vaginal delivery breech birth, but this is not strictly necessary.

The external turning of your baby can be effective but it is not without risks and should be attempted only by an experienced midwife or physician, who will monitor the baby's heartbeat as he is being turned.

The natural way

In order to avoid having to make these decisions about this kind of medical intervention, there are several natural procedures you might like to consider that may assist in turning your baby before the birth.

There has been a suggestion that spending 15 minutes every two hours of the waking day in the knee-chest position will help the baby to turn (known as Elkin's manoeuvre).

There is some evidence that hypnotherapy may be useful, although only one study has looked at this. Acupuncture has been suggested as an effective therapy for turning breech babies and the results of a formal study are awaited.

Older midwives recommend massaging your belly with almond oil for ten minutes while lying on your back with your hips higher than your head. Before you start this regime, ask your midwife which way your baby is most likely to turn so that you can massage in the correct direction.

A Canadian study has shown that classical music might be able to turn a breech baby. Headphones were placed on the mother's lower abdomen and calming classical music was played for an hour each day over a five-day period. Often the baby turns towards the source of the music.

Finally, there is anecdotal evidence to suggest that swimming may help a baby to turn. There is no scientific explanation for this but some believe it's due to the double buoyancy of the mother and baby in the water.

Breaking Waters

Some doctors or midwives perform artificial rupture of membranes (ARM or breaking the waters) to speed up labour if it's progressing slowly. This procedure can be done during an internal examination. A midwife or doctor makes a small break in the membranes around your baby, using either an amniohook (a long thin probe that looks a little like a fine crochet hook) or an amnicot (a medical glove with a pricked end on one of the fingers). This procedure often works when the cervix feels soft and ready for labour to start.

However, ARM does not always work, and, once your waters have been broken, your baby could be at risk of infection. Moreover, it only shortens labour by about an hour but it does tend to increase pain as the baby's head is now directly on the cervix. This can lead to the need for more pain relief and possibly more interventions.

Birthing in water is a good way to minimize the risk of ARM because the pressure of the water often helps to do this naturally. There is debate among midwives about whether a baby should be allowed to be born without the membranes breaking. Some believe it can cushion the head through the birth canal and poses no danger to the baby. Others believe ARM is necessary to check that there is no meconium (waste from the first bowel movement) in the amniotic fluid, which can indicate that the baby is in distress.

Monitoring

In hospitals, your baby's heartbeat is generally monitored throughout labour so that any problems with the baby are able to be detected at the earliest possible moment. This usually involves attaching you to a monitor via a belt or pads placed on the abdomen, and the baby's heartbeat is then recorded on screen. The other, less common form of monitoring involves placing an electrode on the baby's scalp via the vagina.

Either method is restrictive. If you want to move freely, you will have to ask your attendant to monitor intermittently rather than continuously. Alternatively, you can request that your baby's heart rate be monitored using an electronic stethoscope (Doppler) or a fetoscope, just as it would be if you were having a home delivery.

Induction

If the birth of your baby is more than two weeks overdue, your medical team will probably want to induce you. The methods of induction of labour normally offered by medical staff are membrane sweeping, which is a drug-free intervention (see right), prostaglandin gel or pessaries, which are inserted into the vagina (or occasionally given orally), artificial rupture of the membranes (see pages 143–4), and an oxytocin drip, which is given in the synthetic forms of Syntocinon (in the UK) and Pitocin (in the USA).

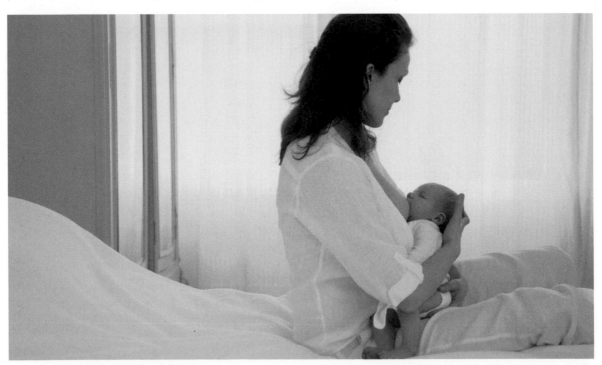

The natural way

Holistic therapies, such as homeopathy, acupuncture, reflexology, aromatherapy, flower essences and herbal remedies, have all been known to give good results in starting labour.

Many traditional self-help methods for inducing labour are still used in traditional societies. The evidence for their efficacy tends to be anecdotal but support for the following methods persists:

- Lots of moderate exercise
- Sexual intercourse
- Eating spicy food, such as curry
- Taking a car ride down a bumpy road
- Nipple stimulation for at least an hour (you could use a breast pump rather than doing it manually)
- Eating lots of fresh pineapple
- Drinking raspberry leaf or cumin tea
- Adding a few drops of clary sage and jasmine essential oil to a bath

WARNING Herbal, aromatherapy and homeopathic self-help measures are extremely potent and are dangerous if used without the advice of a trained practitioner.

- Drinking 3 teaspoons of castor oil mixed in a glass of orange juice (Note: castor oil can give you cramps and diarrhoea – use with great caution)
- Taking herbal remedies blue cohosh or goldenseal
- Taking the homeopathic remedy Caulophyllum 30c and Gelsemium

Note: It is worth bearing in mind that complementary therapies and self-help measures to induce labour are still an intervention, albeit usually a gentler one than hospital induction. Nonetheless, you are interfering with your body's natural rhythms and ability to give birth at the right time for you, so you should think through why exactly you are doing this. If it's about avoiding a hospital induction, then a natural route to starting labour can be just as effective.

Tearing and Episiotomy

When your vagina does not stretch enough, or the baby comes out too quickly, a tear in the perineum can occur. If, during the labour, your doctor or midwife suspects this may happen to you, they will probably suggest an episiotomy (a small cut from the vagina towards the anus) under local anaesthetic. The cut, or a tear, are then sutured (stitched) after the birth.

There are those in the holistic field who believe that it is preferable to tear naturally rather than to have an episiotomy, since a natural tear is thought to heal more quickly.

The natural way

Undoubtedly, it is better if you can avoid tearing or an episiotomy altogether, and there are several measures you can take to help prevent this.

Perineal massage during your pregnancy is often recommended as a way to prepare your vaginal canal for birth and to prevent tearing, although the evidence suggests this helps with superficial tearing only. Vitamin E oil or almond oil with chamomile or calendula added are excellent oils for perineal massage.

Lovemaking is another good way to tone and prepare your uterus and vaginal muscles for the birth.

During the birth, some midwives use oil poured on the perineal area to lubricate and prevent tearing. There are also precautions you can take to help yourself. As the baby's head begins to emerge, you'll feel a stretching or stinging sensation in your vagina. At this point, try to resist pushing and adopt rapid, short, panting breaths or blowing so that the baby exits slowly. Most midwives agree that taking time at this stage is the best way to prevent tearing – they may also encourage you to lie on your left side as this seems to be the optimum position to deliver slowly and without tearing.

Recently, midwives and doulas (see page 150) have started to recommend that you draw your legs together and rock your hips from side to side, as if rocking your baby, at this crowning stage of the birth to prevent delivering the baby too quickly, which causes tearing.

Caesarean

Once the effects of the anaesthetic have worn off, you can experience some pain after a Caesarean section. Many midwives recommend mild analgesics to take the edge off the pain so you can nurse your baby.

The natural way

Midwives encourage breast-feeding after a Caesarean because it produces endorphins that will ease the pain. When breast-feeding, try placing a pillow over your stomach to support the baby and protect the sore area.

Be careful not to pull or strain your abdominal or stomach muscles. Sleeping on your side supported by large pillows may help. Flower and homeopathic remedies can bring gentle relief from both physical and emotional problems after a Caesarean section. If you feel weepy, which is common, try Arnica 6c or Rescue Remedy to help stabilize your emotions.

Natural Pain Relief

None of us can know how we are going to cope with the pain of labour, especially if this is a first baby. Yet knowledge is power and if you are aware of the various methods of pain relief that are available, you can approach the coming birth feeling confident and positive about how you will deal with the pain.

If you are keen to avoid the use of conventional drugs or anaesthetics, then the following natural pain relief methods are not only effective but they can also help you to enjoy a natural and wondrous birth.

Acupuncture

Whether at home or in a medical setting, an acupuncture practitioner in attendance at the birth can be very helpful for managing painful contractions and backache. Needles may be inserted in the ear in order to trigger the release of endorphins, the body's natural pain killers, and it takes about half an hour for the build-up to become effective. Acupoints on your lower back and spine may also be stimulated

in order to ease back pain and on the hand to make the contractions more effective.

TENS

A TENS (Transcutaneous Electrical Nerve Stimulation) machine works along similar principles to acupuncture but can be administered either yourself or by your birthing partner. Electrodes in pads are attached to acupoints on your lower back and a pulsed electric current blocks pain messages from the cervix and uterus to the brain. The current is controlled by a hand-held control device, so you can move around with ease, increasing or reducing the intensity of the current with the contractions.

TENS seems to work best and give you the most effective pain relief if you start using it at the very beginning of your labour. It takes about an hour for your body to respond to the electrical impulses by releasing endorphins, so start using it as soon as you begin to get contractions or backache. Start with the controls at their lowest settings and turn them up gradually as your contractions or the back pain gets stronger. Use the boost button at the peak of contractions.

Warmth and Water

Warmth from a wrapped hot-water bottle or wheat bag placed on your back, tummy or groin can help to relieve the pain of labour.

Taking a warm bath is known to make contractions more bearable, which is why some women book a complete water birth. And there is clinical evidence to support the increasing number of women who opt for this birth experience. A study by the Oxford Centre for Health Care Research and Development in 2001, showed that the need for pain-relieving narcotics and epidurals was significantly lower when women labour in a birthing pool.

In light of this and other research evidence, in September 2007, the UK Government's health watchdog, NICE, recommended that all expectant mothers should be offered a water birth for the safest form of pain relief. NICE states that birthing pools are second only to epidurals in alleviating pain.

Some women view a birthing pool as a form of pain relief that can be tried before resorting to other medical alternatives, if necessary. In fact, you can quite easily take gas and air (see page 149) while in a birthing pool if you should wish to combine the two.

Breathing

Focusing on your breathing is an effective and safe way of getting through each contraction.

At the beginning of the contraction, take a deep breath in through your nose.

As you breathe out through your mouth, visualize the pain and tension ebbing away from your body and actively relax.

You don't have to breathe too deeply – just concentrate on keeping a good rhythm going.

Repeat again and again, keeping your face, jaw and mouth soft. Concentrate fully on your breathing as the contraction builds up, and as it fades away.

When the contraction is over, relax.

Massage

Since time immemorial, massage has been one of the simplest yet most effective ways to relieve pain during labour.

You can tell your birth partner or midwife where and how you'd like to be massaged; slow rhythmical movements tend to ease tension and firmer strokes can stimulate you when your energies are flagging, especially during a lengthy labour.

Hypnotherapy

Self-hypnosis techniques have proven so successful in helping to control the pain of labour that it is now a recognized birthing option known as hypnobirthing (or the Mongan Method).

A course of antenatal hypnobirthing lessons teaches you simple but powerful self-hypnosis techniques to induce feelings of relaxation and peace during labour and birth. The aim is to help release any fears and anxieties that naturally affect many pregnant women, either in the run-up to their first experience of labour and birth or those who have had previous traumatic births. The emphasis is very much on the woman staying in control of her own mind and body, rather than feeling helpless and disempowered.

According to Hypnobirthing UK (see Useful Contacts, page 156), a totally pain-free labour cannot be guaranteed. However, it maintains that 65–70 per cent of mothers who use hypnobirthing techniques need no pain relief and that around half of these experience no pain, just pressure. A further 20–25 per cent require a mild form of pain relief, such as gas and air, with the remaining 5–10 per cent needing special intervention for a variety of reasons.

Aromatherapy

A few drops of lavender essential oil can be added to your massage base oil for additional pain relief and relaxation. Chamomile, bergamot, mandarin or frankincense essential oils are great for their calming effect and to relieve anxiety.

Clary sage is often recommended to help improve contractions, but this is a very powerful essential oil and should be prepared in advance by a qualified aromatherapy practitioner and only used under his strict guidance.

Flower Essences

Take Bach Rescue Remedy or mimulus flower remedy if you're feeling fearful or have a sense of rising panic. Rescue Remedy and Star of Bethlehem can be helpful if you feel you are struggling. In the latter stages of labour, mugwort flower remedy is said to promote the birthing process, while walnut can help you to adjust to the rapid physical changes your body is experiencing.

Homeopathy

Consult a qualified homeopath before you go into labour. S/he may recommend certain remedies, such as Aconite 6c, for rapid contractions; Pulsatilla 6c for back pain, Belladonna 6c for sciatic pain (radiating down your back into your thighs) and Gelsemium 6c for abdominal cramps.

CONVENTIONAL PAIN RELIEF

ANAESTHETIC (e.g. epidural) Blocks all pain locally. An epidural is administered by an anaesthetist via a catheter into your spine, to numb the nerves in your uterus and surrounding muscles.

Disadvantages You cannot walk about, your blood pressure may drop, you may have to be catheterized to pass urine, it can slow labour and increase chances of use of forceps or ventouse for delivery, plus there's a small risk of you having a severe headache and a very small risk of nerve damage. In larger doses (more than 100 mcg), these drugs may affect your baby's breathing, or make him drowsy.

INHALED ANALGESICS (e.g. gas and air, also known as entonox) Takes the edge off the pain rather than completely blocking it out and is safe for your baby. Breathed in through a mask at the beginning of a contraction.

Disadvantages It may make you feel slightly light-headed or sick and gives you a dry mouth.

NARCOTICS (e.g. pethidine) These opiates help you to relax and offer some pain relief but not total. Administered via injection in your thigh or bottom.

Disadvantages It may make you feel drowsy or sick and can cross the placenta, making your baby drowsy or, occasionally, affecting his breathing.

Reflexology

Reflex points on the ankle bones correspond to the uterus and pelvis, and can be stimulated to relieve pain and to regulate contractions. During your pregnancy, consult a trained reflexologist to instruct you on where to press during labour.

Doulas

There was once a time when womenfolk within the immediate and extended family – mothers, sisters, grandmothers, aunts – would be on hand to provide a nurturing role for a new mother, to guide her by experience and help with the practicalities before, during and after the birth. This is still the case in certain traditional societies, but in the West this tradition has long since passed. However, a relatively new addition to the childbirth team, the professional doula, is reviving this time-honoured role.

If you are not confident that you will get the emotional support you need through the birth, then the services of a birth doula could be useful.

A doula is a professional trained in birth physiology and the dynamics of childbearing. She offers emotional and practical support to an expectant woman before, during and after childbirth. A doula believes in 'mothering the mother' – enabling a woman to have the most satisfying and empowered time that she can during pregnancy, birth and the early days as a new mum.

Although trained and experienced in childbirth (the women who become doulas are often health professionals who want to provide additional services and skills to families), not all doulas have given birth themselves. They have a good knowledge and awareness of female physiology but the doula is not present at the birth in a clinical role – that is the job of the midwife and/or medical staff.

If there are several people providing you with support during the birth (such as your husband or partner and a family member or friend) as well as a doula, make sure that the members of your 'team' all communicate well with each other and that each person is clear about what his or her role will be, so you can remain focused on your labour rather than directing them.

greenfile

Doula (pronounced 'doola') is a Greek word meaning 'woman servant or care giver'.

Birth Doulas

A doula's role is flexible and she will usually fit in with your specific needs or given situation. In broad terms, she may:

- meet you (and your partner and other children) before the birth
- suggest comfort measures, such as breathing, relaxation, movement and positioning during the labour
- encourage your partner's active participation in the birth
- nurture, support and reassure you throughout the birth
- visit you at home once the baby is born

Post-natal Doulas

If you are not able to rely on a good local family and friends support network, then you may consider employing a post-natal doula who specializes in post-partum support.

A post-partum doula's role would usually include both emotional and practical support. She may help with light household duties (laundry, cooking, general tidying-up – you will need to discuss the scope of any domestic duties with her beforehand), she can help with caring for any other children you may have, and she can support breast-feeding (or guide you towards professional breast-feeding support if the need arises). She also encourages mothers to rest or sleep and would look after your newborn during that time.

Post-natal doulas usually work around three or four hours per day every day or every other day for up to six weeks after the birth (or for a period to be agreed between you).

So, if you think your partner, relatives or friends can give you the encouragement and support you need during your labour and birth, but the new baby and housework are getting the better of you,

finding the right person

Once you have found a trained doula and established her credentials (see Useful Contacts, page 156), before appointing her ask yourself the following:

Could we spend up to 48 hours together?

Does she listen to me well?

Will she respect my wishes?

Will my partner (or children if applicable, for a home birth perhaps) like her?

Research shows that having a doula present at a birth:

Shortens first-time labour by an average of 2 hours

Decreases the chance of Caesarean section by 50 per cent

Decreases the need for pain medication

Helps fathers participate with confidence

Increases success in breast-feeding

perhaps a post-partum doula is a good option for you and will help relieve any stress or anxiety in the early days.

See page 156 for useful contact addresses.

Early Days With Your Baby

So, you have your baby. It's hard to believe that this tiny infant who has been part of you for so long and whose arrival has been eagerly anticipated, is now here. It is the beginning of a new era and a period of adjustment will ensue.

However, don't be surprised if the early days after the birth are not quite as you imagined they would be. Sitting cuddling your new baby, surrounded by congratulation cards and flowers, you may find yourself experiencing a range of emotions from elation to sheer terror, indifference to distaste. Some women are lucky enough to sail through the birth, to bond instantly with their baby and to take the whole business in their stride. But, in the early days, the majority find themselves preoccupied with more basic and pressing compulsions, such as wanting to urinate without pain, dreading the first bowel movement and juggling with breast-feeding.

Bonding

Although you may imagine that love for your new baby will be instantaneous, most parents do not feel love at first sight. However, the mothering instinct to

greenfile

A great way to aid bonding is to give your baby a regular massage, which is relaxing and pleasurable for you both. Bathing him, breast- or bottle-feeding where applicable, or simply cuddling and talking to him also aid the bonding process.

cuddle and protect, if not love, your baby is very strong. In the early days, when you're just getting to know each other, your baby's utter dependence on you will be enough to get you up in the middle of the night in response to his cries.

As time passes and you go about the daily routine of caring for your baby, the bonding process often takes place unnoticed and it's not until your baby smiles at you and your heart melts that you realize bonding has occurred naturally.

The bonding process may take a little longer if you've had a particularly traumatic birth, you're depressed, your baby is in an incubator or needs special care, or if he is handicapped. Some parents simply find it difficult to relate to their baby until he starts to become more responsive and interactive. In fact, there's no single right time to bond with your baby; it's all about building a loving and trusting relationship.

The most important thing to remember is that the bond almost invariably happens sooner or later but it is less likely to take place if you are tense, depressed or feeling guilty about your initial reactions. The more you worry about not falling in love, the harder it is to achieve.

Feeding

How you feed your baby is a highly emotive topic but it is a decision that you alone can take.

Breast-feeding It is well recognized that breast milk meets your baby's needs perfectly and is digested easily; but your baby won't suffer unduly if you decide

---

greenfile

If you experience discomfort or pain when your milk comes in, there are a few simple green remedies that might help you:

• If your breasts are engorged, place a cold cabbage leaf (straight from the fridge) inside your bra to ease the pain, and inhale a couple of drops of jasmine oil on a tissue.

• The homeopathic remedy Belladonna is recommended but check with a qualified homeopath for the correct dosage.

• Drinking sage tea or taking capsules may help reduce engorgement.

If engorgement develops and it's too painful to breast-feed, try to empty your breasts yourself using a breast pump or hand expressing methods to prevent mastitis (inflammation of the breasts) setting in.

Remember, once you've started with full bottle-feeding you can't switch to breast-feeding. Your body will stop producing milk without the stimulation of your baby sucking at the breast.

Despite it being the natural option, breast-feeding can take some time and patience to master. Midwives are excellent at offering help in the early days but if you're still struggling when their visits have ceased, you could contact your local branch of the La Leche League or NCT, both of whom have breast-feeding counsellors who can help you personally (see Useful Contacts, page 156).

get longer stretches of uninterrupted sleep in the early days but bear in mind that a bottle-feed takes longer to deliver and you need to prepare the bottles and warm the milk.

Whichever method of feeding you decide upon, remember that the closeness, love, cuddling and attention that the baby receives at this special time are just as important as the milk that you give him. A relaxed feeding time will provide deep contentment for both you and your baby.

to bottle-feed. Feeding your baby should be a pleasure, not a challenge, and it won't be if you breast-feed from a sense of obligation, or bottle-feed while feeling guilty. Don't let anyone make you feel bad about your choice – it's a highly personal issue.

It is scientifically proven that there is no substitute for the colostrum that your breasts produce in the first few days. Breast-feeding your baby will provide him with the valuable antibodies essential for fighting infection in the early months. Even if you feed for a day or two only, it's of benefit to your baby.

Bottle-feeding In some respects, bottle-feeding gives you more freedom and flexibility than breast-feeding: someone else can help with feeds, and fathers often become more involved at an earlier stage with bottle-fed babies. In addition, bottle-fed babies are often able to last longer between feeds, because formula is usually digested more slowly than breast milk. This means that you will probably

Emotional Adjustment

There is usually help on hand to deal with the physical discomforts. What is less forthcoming is help with the emotional bruises. After all, many new mums feel a bit deflated after the nine-month build-up to the main event. Although delighted to have their baby in their arms, many confess to experiencing feelings of anti-climax after so much hype and expectation. Don't feel guilty about any such emotions – tiredness, surging hormones and a normal 'day-after-the-big-event' ennui are usually at the root of it all. Remember, you are still physically and emotionally vulnerable, so don't attempt to put on a brave face for visitors if you are feeling wretched.

Midwives and friends may warn you to expect to feel low and weepy on the third or fourth day after the birth. This is commonly known as the baby blues and it is characterized by crying spells, feelings of

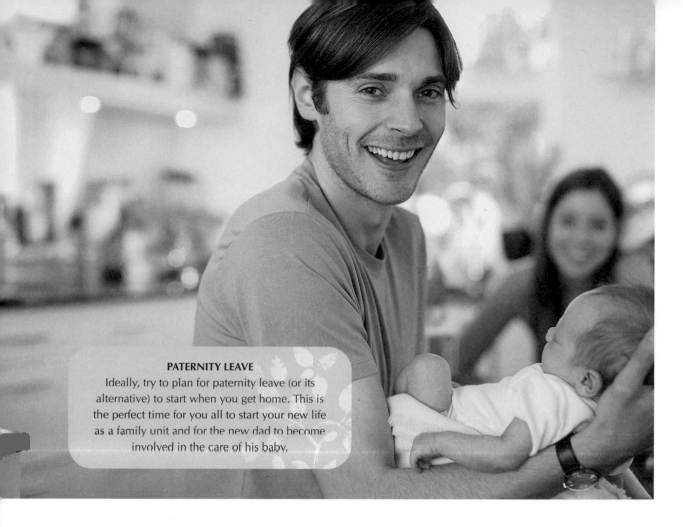

inadequacy and exhaustion. It usually passes very
quickly and relaxation, rest, massage, exercise and
good nutrition can hasten the process. However, if
these feelings persist, you should talk to your midwife,
health visitor or doctor about it.

Heavy bleeding (see page 154), may lead to
anaemia, which can also make you feel tired and low.
Ensure that you inform your healthcare team if you
think you may be anaemic, and continue to eat iron-
rich foods to keep your strength up (see pages 44–5).

*The larch, elm, pine, willow, Star of
Bethlehem and crab apple Bach flower
remedies are excellent for despondent
moments after the birth.*

Family Life

Although the father does not have to cope with the
physical after-effects of the birth, he too may well be
experiencing mixed emotions. Some men report feeling
superfluous and useless during and after the birth and
many lack confidence when it comes to handling their
new baby. Conversely, some fathers automatically take
on a loving and caring role for the newborn, particularly
if the mother is recovering from a hard delivery, and
many are surprised and overcome by the depth of their
emotions for the new baby. Certainly, the emotional
roller coaster that most parents experience in the early
days can put a strain on any relationship. Tolerance
and understanding are essential during this period of
adjustment and if you can discuss your feelings with
one another, you are far more likely to weather any
changes that may affect your relationship.

Useful Contacts

A Healthy Start

The Royal College of Nursing
www.rcn.org.uk
Publishes the booklet 'Sensitive Disposal Of All Fetal Remains – Guidance For Nurses And Midwives'.

British Wheel of Yoga
www.bwy.org.uk
National governing body for yoga.

British Meditation Society
www.britishmeditationsociety.org
Non-profit making meditation organization.

General Council for Massage Therapies
www.gcmt.org.uk
The governing body for massage therapies and all bodyworks and soft tissue techniques in the UK.

National Childbirth Trust (NCT)
www.nct.org.uk
Support for parents during pregnancy, birth and early days of parenthood.
Pregnancy & Birth Helpline: 0300 330 0772
Breast-feeding Helpline: 0300 330 0771
Enquiries: 0300 330 0770

NHS Direct
www.nhsdirect.nhs.uk
Health advice and information.
Helpline: 0845 4647

Maternity Action
www.maternityaction.org.uk
Advice to pregnant women and new parents.

The Miscarriage Association
www.miscarriageassociation.org.uk
Providing support and information for those suffering the effects of pregnancy loss.
Helpline: 01924 200799

Healthy Eating

Eating for Pregnancy
www.eatingforpregnancy.co.uk
Advice on how to optimize your lifestyle and diet to get your baby off to the best possible start.

British Nutrition Foundation
www.nutrition.org.uk
Provides information on food and nutrition in the context of health and lifestyle.

Food Standards Agency
www.food.gov.uk/healthiereating
Advice on healthy eating.

Drinkline – The National Alcohol Helpline
Helpline: 0800 917 8282

Alcoholics Anonymous
www.alcoholics-anonymous.org.uk
Helpline: 0845 769 7555

Royal College of Obstetricians and Gynaecologists
www.rcog.org.uk

Healthy Living

Quitline (smoking)
0800 00 22 00

NHS Pregnancy Smoking Helpline
0800 169 9 169

Narcotics Anonymous
www.ukna.org
Helpline: 0300 999 12 12

Safe Cosmetics
www.safecosmetics.co.uk
Advice, campaigns and DIY recipes for safe, natural cosmetics and toiletries.

Campaign for Safe Cosmetics
www.safecosmetics.org
American site giving advice, campaigns and DIY recipes for safe, natural cosmetics and toiletries.

Environment Agency
www.environment-agency.gov.uk

Drinking Water Inspectorate
www.dwi.gov.uk

Prenatal Care

The Independent Midwives Association
www.independentmidwives.org.uk
Professional organization promoting the role of independent practitioners who choose to work outside the NHS.

National Childbirth Trust (NCT)
www.nct.org.uk
Support for parents during pregnancy, birth and early days of parenthood.
Pregnancy & Birth Helpline: 0300 330 0772
Enquiries: 0300 330 0770

BirthChoice UK
www.birthchoiceuk.com
Information to help you choose where to have your baby.

Association for Improvements in the Maternity Services
www.aims.org.uk
Provides support and information about maternity choices in the UK.

The Royal College of Midwives
www.rcm.org.uk
Information about active birth and your midwife's commitment to supporting your choices in labour.

Lamaze
www.lamaze.org
A non-profit organization that promotes a natural, healthy and safe approach to pregnancy, childbirth and early parenting.

Maternity Services Liaison Committees
www.mslc.org.uk
MSLCs are locally based groups of all those involved in planning, providing and receiving maternity care, including users.

Home Birth Support Groups
www.homebirth.org.uk
Information and opinions about home birth, for parents who think that it might be the right choice for them.

UNICEF UK's Baby Friendly Initiative
www.babyfriendly.org.uk
Working with the healthcare system to ensure a high standard of care for pregnant women and breast-feeding mothers and babies.

Fetal Medicine Foundation
www.fetalmedicine.com
A training and accreditation scheme to maintain standards in nuchal scanning. Look for your nearest private accredited centre.

Antenatal Results and Choices (ARC)
www.arc-uk.org
A charity that supports and offers information to parents throughout the antenatal testing process.
Helpline: 020 7631 0285

Tiny Tickers
www.tinytickers.org
A charity that supports effective cardiac health in obstetrics and gives advice and support to affected parents.

Remedies and Therapies

The Complementary and Natural Healthcare Council
www.cnhc.org.uk
The CNHC is the UK's national regulator for complementary healthcare practitioners.

Association of Reflexologists
www.aor.org.uk

The Aromatherapy Council
www.aromatherapycouncil.co.uk

British Acupuncture Council
www.acupuncture.org.uk
The UK's main regulatory body for the practice of traditional acupuncture.

British Chiropractic Association
www.chiropractic-uk.co.uk
The largest and longest-established association for chiropractors in the UK with an online directory of registered practitioners.

European Central Council of Homeopaths
www.homeopathy-ecch.org
Lists its member associations in each country.

British Homeopathic Association
www.britishhomeopathic.org
The online practitioners listed in your area are all members of the Faculty of Homeopathy.

National Institute of Medical Herbalists
www.nimh.org.uk
The UK's leading professional body representing herbal practitioners.

General Osteopathic Council
www.osteopathy.org.uk
Provides a register of qualified osteopaths for the UK.

The Shiatsu Society
www.shiatsu.org
A non-profit organization that represents all styles of shiatsu and the majority of shiatsu practitioners, schools and students in the UK.

The UK Reiki Federation
www.reikifed.co.uk
For information about reiki. A directory of Reiki Masters is available for a charge.

The UK Confederation of Hypnotherapy Organisations
www.ukcho.co.uk
UKCHO is an umbrella body for the hypnotherapy profession in the UK.

National Council for Hypnotherapy
www.hypnotherapists.org.uk
The largest not-for-profit hypnotherapy organization in the UK, with a therapist finder facility.

Natural Birth Options

Doula UK
www.doula.org.uk
Information about finding a doula.

Doula Directory
www.douladirectory.org.uk
A free-to-use directory.

La Lèche League GB
www.laleche.org.uk
Breast-feeding information, helpline and support.
Helpline: 0845 120 2918

National Childbirth Trust (NCT)
www.nct.org.uk
Support for parents during pregnancy, birth and early days of parenthood.
Pregnancy & Birth Helpline: 0300 330 0772
Breast-feeding Helpline: 0300 330 0771
Enquiries: 0300 330 0770

Hypnobirthing UK
www.hypnobirthing.co.uk
Information and how to find a practitioner.

Index